# BEGINNERS GUITAR JUMPSTART

Learn Basic Chords, Rhythms and Strum Your First Songs

ANDY SCHNEIDER

**Listen to This Book!**

*Download the free audio examples of these exercises*

Scan and go now

**SEEINGMUSICBOOKS.COM**

## SEEING MUSIC
### METHOD BOOKS

© 2019, 2023 ANDY SCHNEIDER
WWW.ANDYSCHNEIDER.COM

## Introduction

I love learning. I love getting new skills that give me new abilities. And, I love passing on those skills to others so that they can enjoy their own talents and new abilities. This book is for the absolute beginner. Welcome.

It's always a good time to start learning music and the guitar. Students of any age can see real results from a good practice routine. Many, many adults and children have benefitted from my teaching method and I hope you'll soon have new abilities to make your own music.

In my years teaching guitar and talking with other professional string players, I've noticed that we all have developed an ability to "see" the music we play on the fretboard of the instrument. We see the music we play as a simple relationship of shapes and relative positions. Look at these two shapes:

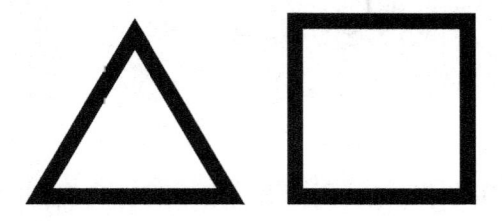

△ □

Just as you recognize the shapes above, stringed instrumentalists see music on the fretboard of their instrument. This is an inherently special gift we who play stringed instruments have been given. No other kind of instrument makes it so easy for the musician to have a visual roadmap of the music, making things like improvisation or transposing a song to another key so easy. Our fingers follow these maps to get to the music. This book will show you how to see music as simple shapes and use these shapes to more quickly and proficiently play and create music.

We'll be covering how music is constructed and 'looks' on the neck of the guitar. While we won't get into any particular musical style or specific techniques, the information here is common to all Western music: Rock, Folk, Country, Pop, Classical, Jazz.

While the first steps of guitar playing are the same for everyone, the next few steps of learning chords can be taught many different ways. I'm going to walk you through what I believe is the fastest and most powerful way. Learning guitar chords with a visual method makes it so much easier and minimizes memorization. You will develop life-long skills that you will use every day you pick up a guitar.

Turn the page: you're about to "see" music!

# SEEING MUSIC
## METHOD BOOKS

# CONTENTS

**SELECTING YOUR FIRST GUITAR** — 7

**GUITAR CARE AND MAINTENANCE** — 11

**DAY 1 - PROPER PLAYING POSITION** — 13

**FRETBOARD DIAGRAMS** — 15
*A NOTE ABOUT FRETBOARD DIAGRAMS* — 17

**DAY 2 - PLAYING SINGLE NOTES** — 19
*GOOD FRETTING TECHNIQUE* — 20
*PUTTING IT ALL TOGETHER* — 21
*ABOUT STAFF NOTATION* — 22

**DAY 3 - THE C MAJOR SCALE** — 25
*THE AWESOME POWER OF SCALES* — 25
*HOW TO PLAY THIS SCALE* — 26
*MORE ABOUT MAJOR SCALES* — 26

**DAY 4 - PLAYING YOUR FIRST CHORDS** — 29
*HOW TO PLAY CHORDS* — 29
*E MAJOR AND A MAJOR CHORDS* — 30

**KNOW YOUR GUITAR** — 35

## DAY 5 - PLAYING BARRE CHORDS — 37
*WHAT ARE BARRE CHORDS? — 37*
*B MAJOR BARRE CHORD — 38*

## DAY 6 - G AND C MAJOR — 41
*HOW TO PLAY A G MAJOR SCALE — 41*
*ALL ABOUT SHARPS AND FLATS — 42*
*PLAYING G AND C MAJOR CHORDS — 43*

## KNOW YOUR FRETBOARD (PART I) — 47
*THE FIRST 3 FRETS — 47*
*MEMORIZING THESE EASILY — 48*

## DAY 7 - THE D MAJOR CHORD — 49
*HOW TO PLAY D MAJOR — 49*
*3/4 TIME SIGNATURE — 50*

## DAY 8 - NEW STRUMMING PATTERNS — 53
*WHAT GOES DOWN MUST COME UP — 53*
*HOW TO ADD UPSTROKES — 54*

## KNOW YOUR FRETBOARD (PART II) — 57
*THE FIFTH FRET — 57*
*THE EVIL B STRING — 58*

## DAY 9 - MINOR CHORDS — 61
*HOW TO PLAY E MINOR — 61*
*HOW TO PLAY A MINOR — 62*
*PUTTING CHORD FLAVORS TOGETHER — 62*

## DAY 10 - PLAY YOUR FIRST SONGS    65
### *HOW TO PLAY JINGLE BELLS*    *65*
### *HOW TO PLAY HAPPY BIRTHDAY*    *66*
### *HOW TO PLAY A BLUES SONG*    *67*
### *HOW TO PLAY A ROCK AND ROLL SONG*    *67*
### *ROCK AND ROLL WITH MINOR CHORDS*    *68*

## MILESTONES IN MUSIC    71

## CHORD AND NOTE REFERENCE    73

# BEGINNERS GUITAR JUMPSTART

# SELECTING YOUR FIRST GUITAR

There are many choices to be made when picking a new guitar. Not only are there different looks, but there are different sizes and designs that affect tone and playability. No one guitar works for all musicians. It's also tricky to know what you'll prefer in a few months or years as you develop as a musician. Let's look at some of the biggest factors guitar buyers face so you can find a great one to play for many years to come.

## *Acoustic or Electric*

You probably have a good idea which one you'd like to own first. Acoustic guitars are versatile and can make music anywhere. Electric guitars are great, but you'll probably want an amplifier, too. So leave a little in your budget for that. There are many inexpensive practice amps that will work just fine.

## *Size and Playability*

This bit is crucial. Guitars come in many sizes, often described by their scale length. *Scale* is literally the length of the string, measured from the bridge to the nut (see chapter *Know Your Guitar* for details). If you're a smaller person, you may want to look for a 3/4 or even 1/2 scale guitar. While solidbody electric guitars all have similar size bodies, acoustics have many different body styles that vary in size. Some of the body styles, from smallest to largest, include parlor, dreadnaught and jumbo. Again, if you're smaller you may want to stay away from bigger bodies. Also, larger bodies have a bit more bass tone, while small bodies have less. This won't matter for your study, but your taste might be for one or the other.

Another factor is the playability or *action* of the neck. Action refers to how easily the guitar plays. For good action, the strings must be fairly close to the frets, but not so close they create a buzzing sound. If you're unfamiliar with how good action feels, ask someone with experience for their opinion of your guitar candidate. Since the action of most guitars can be adjusted by a technician, if you already own a guitar, you may be able to improve its playability at your local repair shop.

Each time the guitar is outfitted with different gauge strings, the action changes and the guitar will need a little adjustment. This operation is usually refered to as a *set-up* and involves adjusting the height of the strings, the bow of the neck (yes, necks are supposed to be slightly bowed) and sometimes adjusting the string slots in the nut.

## Price

This is a big one, obviously. Some people like to be value-minded and find an inexpensive guitar to begin their study. Some people like to make a big investment right away, buying a beautiful guitar from a well-reputed manufacturer. Perhaps it helps them stay motivated to learn or they view it as an investment. Either way, there are great guitars for beginners at all prices. Generally, more expensive guitars have a better tone and some high-quality features, such as more adjustability for the owner's playing style.

## Body Style: Cutaway or Non-Cutaway

The cutaway is a body style that gives the player access to the upper frets. It's a big notch cut into the body where it meets the neck. While most electric guitars have them, acoustics can have them or not. Many players feel that acoustics without cutaways sound slightly better than those that do have cutaways. Since there's not a big sound difference and you probably won't be playing up on those higher frets for a while, this won't be a big issue.

FIG.1 - GUITAR WITH CUTAWAY

FIG.2 - GUITAR WITHOUT CUTAWAY

## Strings

Most electrics will come with metal strings, but acoustic guitars are grouped by the type of string they use. There are two types: nylon and metal. Nylon strings, not being made from metal, have a much lower tension than metal strings. The bodies of those guitars are built differently and metal strings should never be used on a guitar meant for nylon strings. The higher tension can actually damage the guitar. Classical guitars use nylon strings and are typically plucked with fingers, not a pick. While great for playing individual notes, these guitars are not great for strumming. If you plan to do some strumming or lots of playing with a pick, nylon string guitars may not be a good choice.

## Quality of Tuners

This is a bigger issue than you might think. Good quality tuners turn very smoothly and help keep the guitar in tune. Poor ones make it difficult to tune or even cause the guitar to slip out of tune. If you can, try their feel. If you're buying without being able to try them, know that the cost of the guitar is generally an indicator of the quality. Not always, but generally more expensive guitars come with more high-quality tuners.

## Pickups

Not all guitars have pickups. Many acoustics do not. Of those that do, there is a variety of styles. Acoustics generally use a pickup located inside the bridge, while electric guitars use one, two or three magnetic pickups mounted in the body. Again, cost generally indicates the quality. More pickups means more tonal variety, but shouldn't affect your enjoyment of the guitar.

## Other Fancy Stuff

There's lots of things that get added to guitars to either dress them up or add functionality. Adornments like inlays and binding add visual appeal but not playability. Examples of functional upgrades include tremolo bridges, locking tuners, locking nuts and active electronics. For your first purchase, avoid most of these items. In addition to their added function, they hold added complexity that can make tuning or caring for them more challenging.

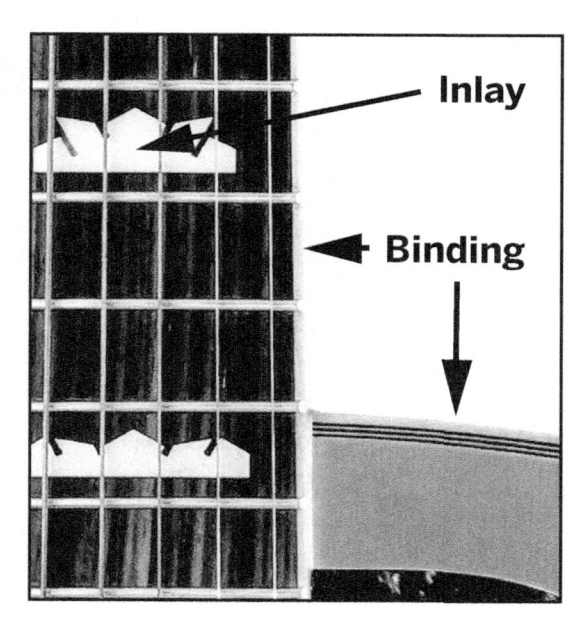

FIG.3 - INLAY AND BINDING

# Keep Learning!
# Join **Seeing Sparks** and Build Your Music Knowledge **FREE**!

Members get free lessons, playing tips, pro interviews and exclusive offers, delivered to your inbox.

The best musicians always are learning.

Scan and go now

# Sign Up Today!

VISIT SEEINGMUSICBOOKS.COM

# SEEING MUSIC METHOD BOOKS

# GUITAR CARE AND MAINTENANCE

## *Storage*

Guitars are a lot like people: They don't like things too hot or too cold, too wet or too dry. Avoid leaving your guitar in very hot or cold places, like a car. A great rule of thumb is, if you would be uncomfortable with the temperature or humidity of a place, don't leave your guitar there.

When putting away your guitar, a hard-shell case is the safest location. A guitar stand is also acceptable. Avoid leaning your guitar against a wall or furniture. If it slips and falls over, it could easily be damaged or broken. Also, avoid leaving it near heaters, radiators or even in bright sunshine.

## *Cleaning*

Keep your guitar clean with guitar polish and a soft rag or polish cloth. Generally, a light spritz of polish and wiping with the polish cloth is all that's necessary. Your guitar's manufacturer may have special recommendations to follow.

## *Replacing Strings*

Strings wear out over time and with use. If you see any discoloration, like rust, or evidence of wear, like dents where the strings meet the frets, buy a new set of strings and have them replaced by a technician. If you're replacing strings yourself, be aware that they can spring up and poke your eyes. Consider wearing safety eyewear. Seriously. Your eyes deserve protection.

FIG.4 - GUITAR ON GUITAR STAND

**GUITAR CARE 11**

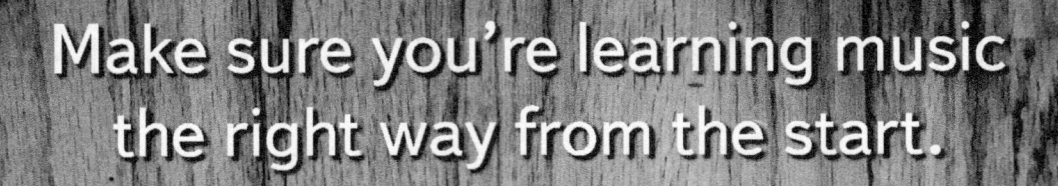

# Make sure you're learning music the right way from the start.

- Learn Your First Bass Lines Quickly
- Learn Many Rhythm Patterns
- Learn Basic Music Concepts and Terms
- Includes First-Time Bass Guitar Buyer's Guide
- Learn Fingerstyle and Pick Techniques

**SEEING MUSIC METHOD BOOKS**

Learn Basic Lines, Rhythms and Play Your First Songs

# BASS GUITAR BEGINNERS JUMPSTART

ANDY SCHNEIDER

BEGINNER

Scan to learn more

See more music.
SeeingMusicBooks.com

**SEEING MUSIC METHOD BOOKS**

**12 BEGINNERS GUITAR JUMPSTART: A SEEING MUSIC METHOD BOOK**

# DAY 1 - PROPER PLAYING POSITION

## *Lay a Great Foundation*

Great music begins with correct posture and instrument position. Start from a sitting position in a chair that allows your upper legs to be parallel to the ground. Hold the guitar close to your body, with the neck pointing slightly upward so your left hand is approximately level with your right elbow. If the neck sags too low to the floor, you'll have to reach farther with your left hand and playing will be difficult and uncomfortable.

Fig.5 - Proper Guitar Position

Fig.6 - Good Hand Position

To aid this, you may want to raise your right heel so the guitar rises up about an inch. Notice in the pictures how the left thumb is directly behind the neck and the wrist is straight. A straight wrist is essential for good technique, but also the hardest part for many students to achieve. In the next chapter, we'll see why.

Whatever you do, don't worry about trying to look cool. Lots of pro rock stars are known for wearing their guitar really low, or slouching, or even jumping in the air. While you're learning the fundamentals, the more time you spend focused on correct posture and technique, the faster you'll get where you want to go. In fact, refer to this chapter often. Remember to always check your alignment and return to good hand and body position if they slip.

The guitar is tuned, low to high, E, A, D, G, B and E. If you're experienced you can tune by ear, but the easiest way to tune is to buy an electronic guitar tuner. Many are available inexpensively. Alternatively, there are lots of great guitar tuners available for phones and tablets. Many of these apps are free, so if you have a smart device, check its app store.

The strings of the guitar are numbered from the highest pitch to the lowest. The highest and lightest string is the first string and the lowest and heaviest string is the sixth string.

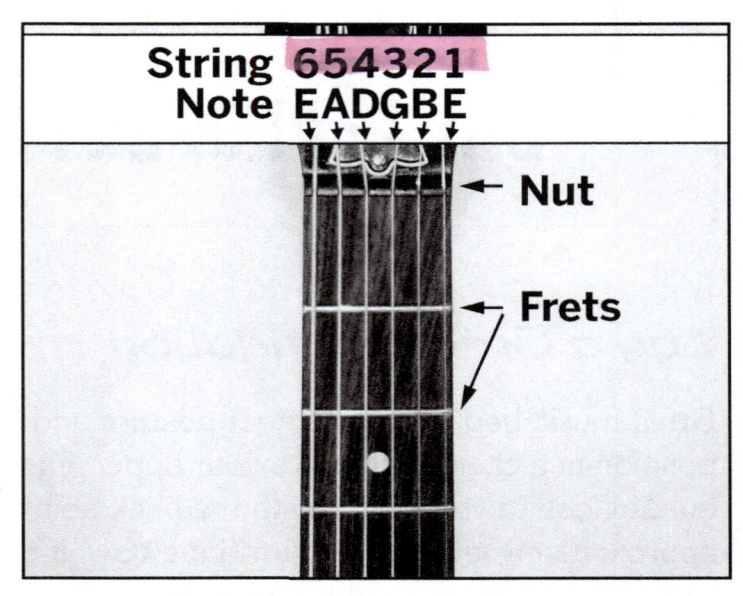

FIG.7 - STRING NAMES AND NUMBERS

## A Note About Fingernails

Long fingernails and guitar playing don't really go well together. If you've got long nails on your fretting hand, you'll find they get in the way of good finger position. They also tend to dig in the wood of the fretboard. Long nails on the picking hand tend to get scuffed or interfere with fingerstyle picking. While long nails may look pretty, you may have to make a tough choice to cut them.

# Thinking of learning banjo, too?

From the jump.. Learn the fun and easy way!

Download the audio examples now for free.
**SEEINGMUSICBOOKS.COM**

# FRETBOARD DIAGRAMS

## How to Read Fretboard Diagrams

You're ready to start learning some notes. The diagrams in this book are kind of like pictures of what you'll see when you look at your guitar.

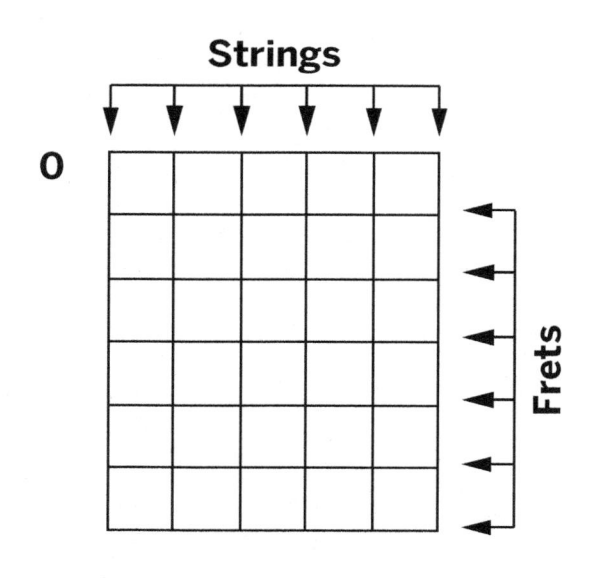

FIG.8 - FRET NOTATION

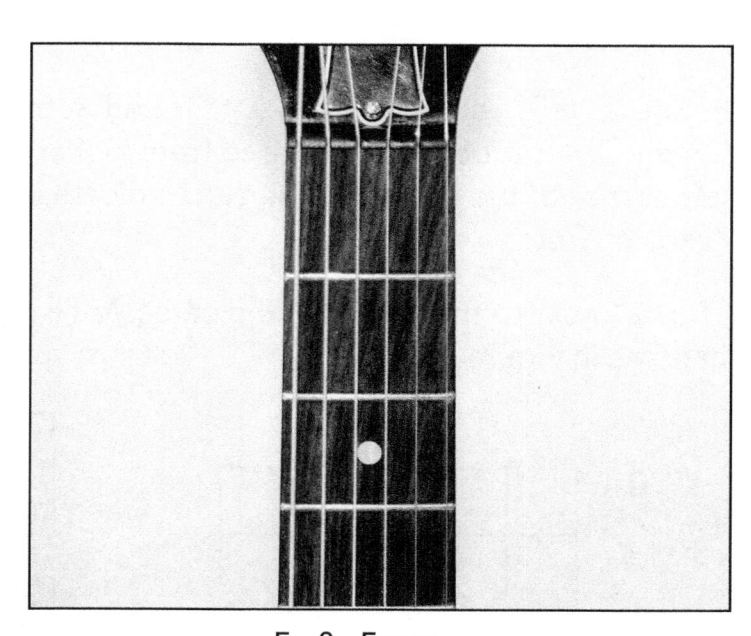

FIG.9 - FRETBOARD

Hold your guitar upright in front of you and look at fretboard. The strings run up and down, the frets run horizontally. That is the view used in fretboard diagrams.

Let's try playing our first note. As indicated in Figure 10, play open E, the 6th string. An open circle indicates an open string, one that is played without fretting with the left hand.

With your picking hand, feel free to use a pick or just your thumb. For now, do whatever is comfortable.

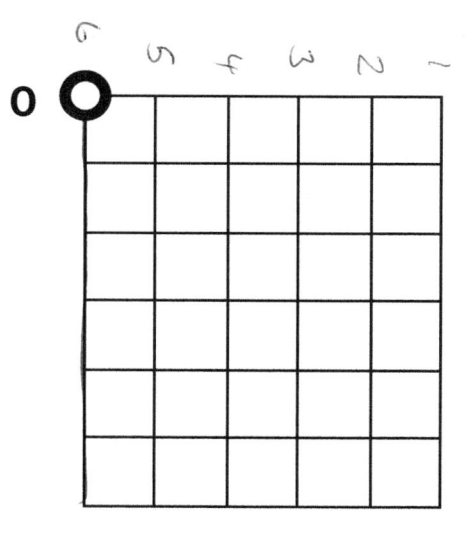

FIG.10 - OPEN 6TH STRING

FIG.11 - OPEN 5TH STRING

Did that go well? Try another, this time open A, the 5th string.

Figure 12 tells you to play the note found at the black dot on the 5th String at the 3rd fret. It's the 3rd fret because it's three frets higher up the neck than the "0" in the upper-left corner of the diagram. The zero indicates that the diagram begins at the nut or "zeroth" fret.

The "2" next to the black dot indicates you'll use your second finger of your fretting hand as in Figure 13.

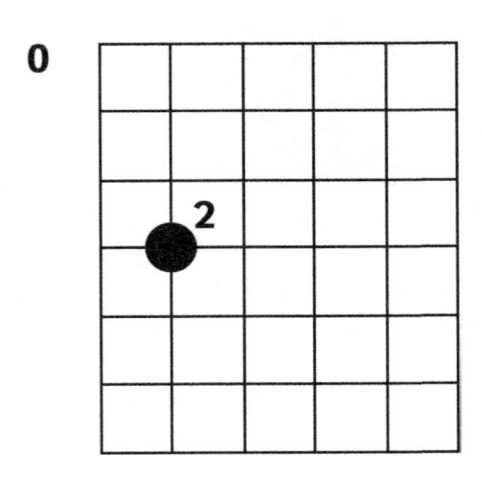

FIG.12 - FRET NOTATION

FIG.13 - LEFT-HAND FINGERING

On these diagrams, a filled in circle indicates that you'll put your finger at that fret. Actually, you'll put your finger just behind the fret, not right on top of the fret. The fret, not your finger, is what stops the vibration of the string and changes its length.

Keeping your finger pressed with medium pressure, just behind the fret will produce the clearest and best sound.

Don't confuse a fretboard diagram with a musical staff. Music staves indicate pitch and rhythm. Fretboard diagrams like Figure 12 are like a roadmap, showing you where to place your fingers.

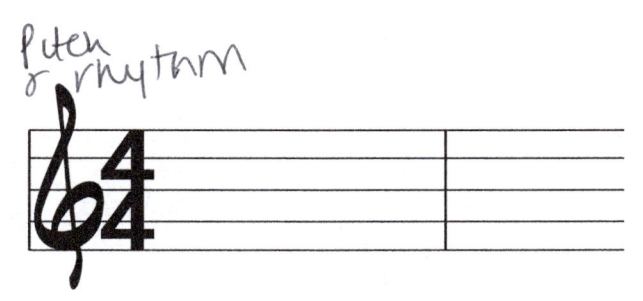

FIG.14 - MUSICAL STAFF

## A NOTE ABOUT FRETBOARD DIAGRAMS

Most other books place the dot in-between the fret lines. While this is a common convention, it's best to think of the notes as located at the intersection of a string and a fret. When you see a dot in this book, you'll know that it is showing you the note to be played and that you'll place your finger just behind that fret to hear it.

## SOUNDCHECK

Fretboard diagrams indicate where to find a note and what finger to use to play it.

The number in the upper-left corner of a fretboard diagram indicates on which fret the diagram begins.

Fretboard diagrams should not be confused with musical staves.

**Listen to This Book!**

Download the free audio examples of these exercises

Scan and go now

SEEINGMUSICBOOKS.COM

FRETBOARD DIAGRAMS 17

# Make sure you're learning music the right way from the start.

- Learn Your First Chords Quickly
- Learn Many Rhythm Patterns
- Learn Basic Music Concepts and Terms
- Includes First-Time Banjo Buyer's Guide
- Photos of Fingerings from *Your* Point-of-View

**SEEING MUSIC METHOD BOOKS**

*Learn Basic Chords, Rhythms and Pick Your First Songs*

# BANJO BEGINNERS JUMPSTART

ANDY SCHNEIDER

BEGINNER

Scan to learn more

See more music.
SeeingMusicBooks.com

**SEEING MUSIC METHOD BOOKS**

**18 BEGINNERS GUITAR JUMPSTART: A SEEING MUSIC METHOD BOOK**

# DAY 2 - PLAYING SINGLE NOTES

||||||||||||||||||||||||||||||||||||||||||||||||||||||||||||||||||||||||

## MILESTONE

*As you pass each milestone, take a moment to recall previous lessons.*

**Have a seat with your guitar in good playing position.**

||||||||||||||||||||||||||||||||||||||||||||||||||||||||||||||||||||||||

Ready to start making music? Let's start with some open string notes.

You'll remember these notes from yesterday's lesson about the names of the strings. Start by playing open E. Using either your right-hand thumb or a pick, sound open E on the 6th string. This is the lowest note on the guitar and maybe the most fun to play!

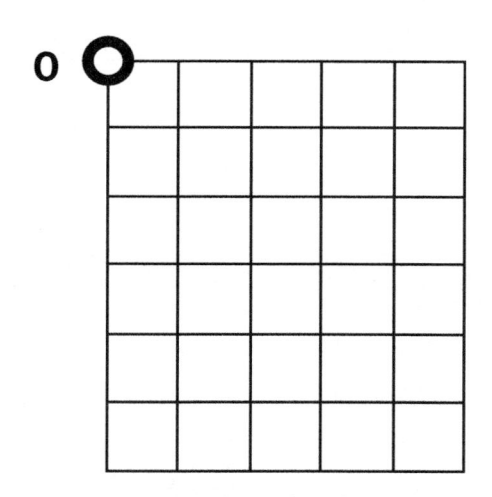

FIG.15 - OPEN 6TH STRING (E) 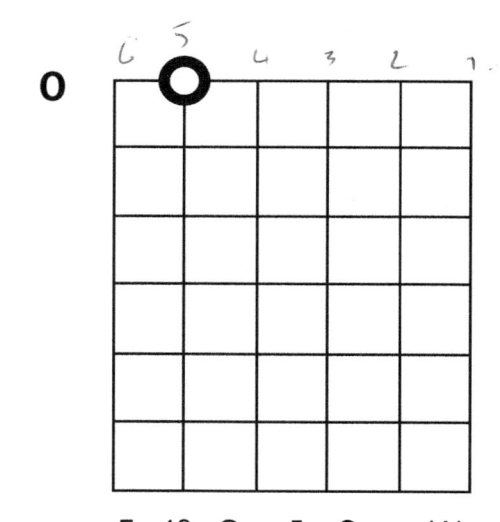    FIG.16 - OPEN 5TH STRING (A)

Now try open A. Feel free to look down at your right hand so you cleanly sound just the 5th string. It's easy to hit other strings in the process, so keep focused on just hitting the A string.

## GOOD FRETTING TECHNIQUE

You've also already played C on the 5th string. Give it a try, using your 2nd finger.

FIG. 17 - 5TH STRING C

On the 6th string, the 3rd fret is G. Use the 2nd finger of your fretting hand on the 3rd fret, as well.

Now repeat, playing C on the 5th string, then G on the 6th. Do this a few more times.

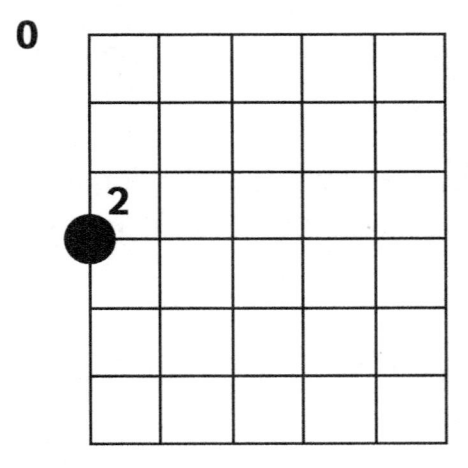

FIG. 18 - 6TH STRING G

## SOUNDCHECK

Now, how do things sound? Are you getting any buzzes? Is the note full and ringing? Most students need several days of this exercise before the notes sound clean and pleasant. If you're having trouble, make certain that your fretting finger is very near the fret. This is crucial. In fact, you'll be so close that you're almost on top of the fret. When you get the feel of it, it will make everything else easier. Keep trying!

Also, keep your wrist straight, not bent. Remember that tilting the neck up and keeping the fretboard near your shoulder will make this easier. Playing guitar should never be uncomfortable, so if your fingers, hands, arms or anywhere else starts to hurt, stop right away. Sometimes fingertips get sore after a practice session, especially if a player is just starting out. In time, callouses develop, making playing less uncomfortable.

## *PUTTING IT ALL TOGETHER*

Every note has a beginning and an end, right? While there's only one way to pick a string, there are two ways to stop it. Let's put it all together, starting and stopping each of the four notes.

Play open A, then open E. Start each note with your pick or thumb, then stop each note by lightly touching the strings with your left fingers. Try it again, picking the note, then "catching" the strings to stop the note.

Similarly, pick C then G. These are fretted notes, so if you let up the pressure with your fretting hand, the note will stop ringing. Give it a try. Tinker with the speed and pressure change with your fretting hand until the note stops cleanly.

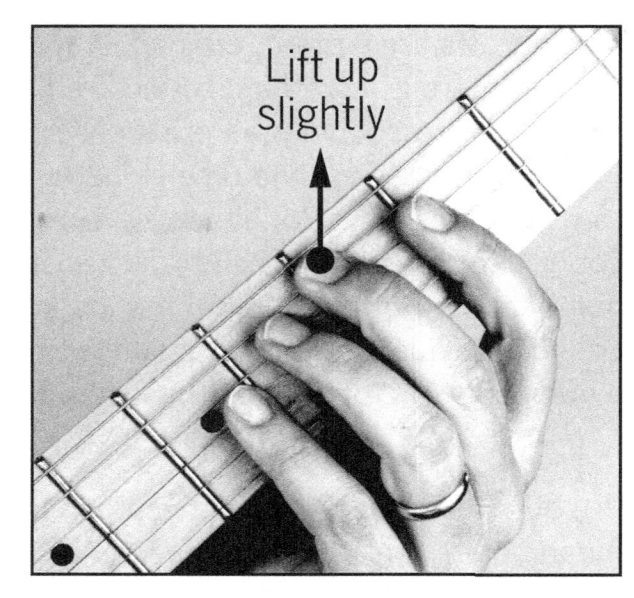

FIG.19 - LEFT-HAND MUTING

Ok, now let's stop these notes a different way. This time, you'll use your picking hand to stop the note. This is called palm muting and it's like putting the brakes on a car. You'll use the bottom of your picking hand, the soft bottom edge of your hand that's between your pinky and wrist. Pick a note, then use your palm's edge to stop it. Is the note stopping cleanly? See how fast you can go from picking the note to stopping it. See how slowly you can do the same. Pretty neat, huh?

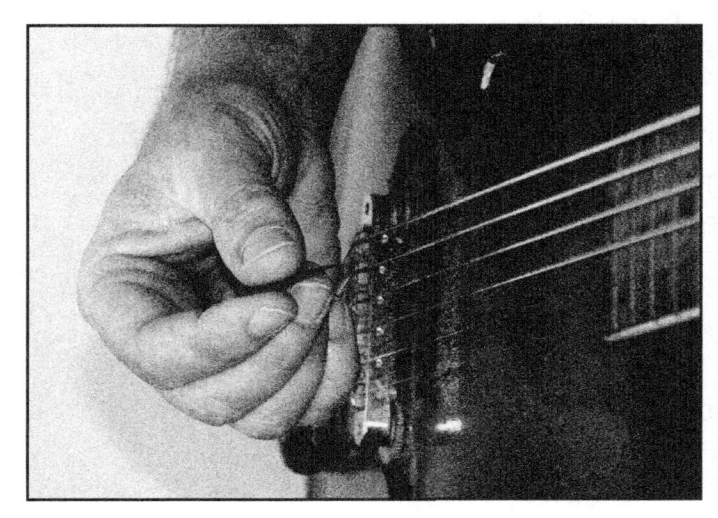

FIG.20 - PICKING POSITION

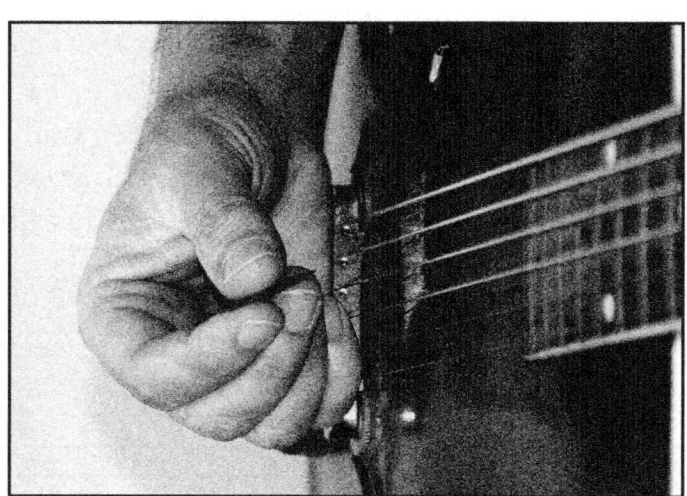

FIG.21 - PALM MUTING

# ABOUT STAFF NOTATION

Music staffs are a great, efficient way to describe rhythm. Here is a staff indicating Treble Clef and time signature. Treble Clef means it's describing upper notes (not bass notes) and the time signature tells us how to count. Most, but not all, music is in 4, meaning we count one measure "1, 2, 3, 4." The top number 4 is that number. The bottom number means that what we are counting is quarter notes. Just as with apples or dollars, a quarter is 1/2 of a half. A half is 1/2 of a whole.

FIG.22 - 4/4 TIME SIGNATURE

So, our staff here indicates we are in the Treble Clef. The song is in 4/4 time, which means there are 4 beats of quarter notes in each measure. A measure is indicated by the vertical lines on the staff.

Figure 23 shows a quarter-note rest. Where notes (or in this book, hash marks) tell us when to play, rests tell us when not to play. Take a little rest!

FIG.23 - QUARTER-NOTE REST

## ASSIGNMENT

### Today's Assignment

Let's practice starting and stopping notes cleanly. The hash marks on the staff tell you when to play a note, the name of the note is above it. The rests tell you when to mute the strings for silence.

Rhythm Tip: Slowly say "One, Two, Three, Four". Now, say the same thing, but whisper on "Two" and "Four". It should sound like "ONE, two, THREE, four". Now, imitate that with your guitar,"ONE, two, THREE, four". Keep repeating this exercise, slowly at first.

**One**  *two*  **Three**  *four*

FIG.24 - COUNTING QUARTER-NOTES AND RESTS

**22 BEGINNERS GUITAR JUMPSTART: A SEEING MUSIC METHOD BOOK**

FIG.25 - E AND A

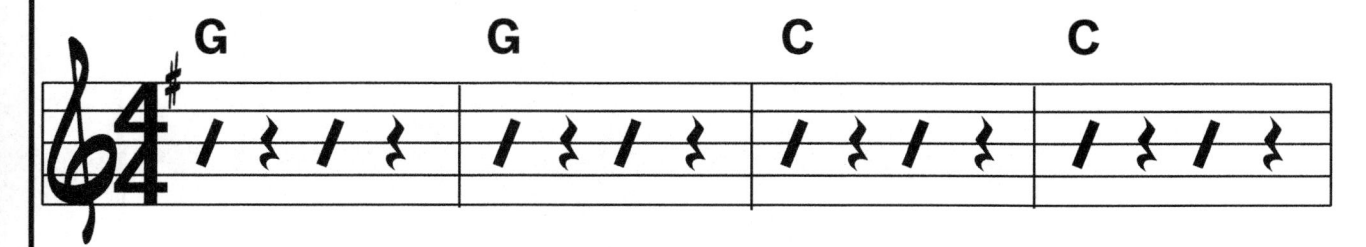

FIG.26 - G AND C

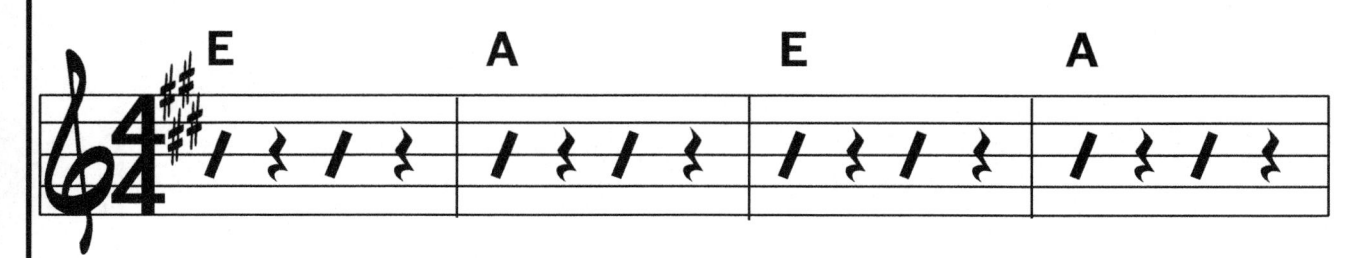

FIG.27 - E AND A ALTERNATING

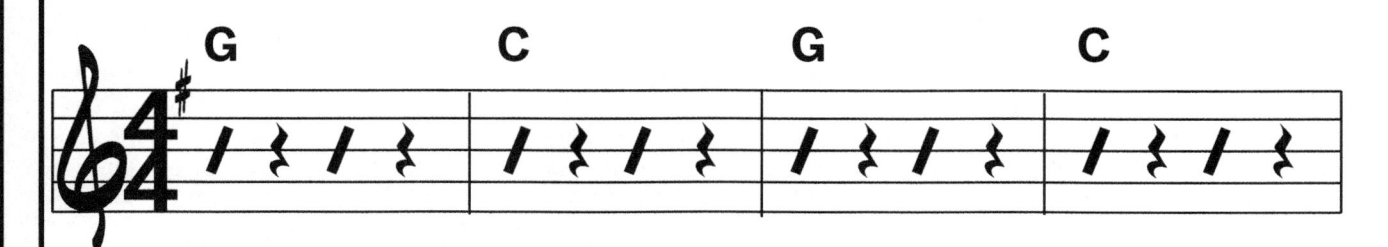

FIG.28 - G AND C ALTERNATING

FIG.29 - C, G, E AND A

**PLAYING SINGLE NOTES**

# DAY 3 - THE C MAJOR SCALE

## MILESTONE

**At the 3rd fret, play C on the 5th string and G on the 6th string.**

**Remember: Your fretting finger should be just behind the fret; the closer, the better.**

### *THE AWESOME POWER OF SCALES*

Scales are awesome because ALL music comes from them! Melodies come from scales. Chords come from scales. And scales are easy to memorize, which will make learning chords easy, too.

Take a look at the C Major scale. The notes of the C Major scale in order are C, D, E, F, G, A, B and C.

# CDEFGABC
Fig.30 - C Major Scale Note Names

All the notes here are separated by a whole-step, except those indicated by the "^" symbol. Those are separated by a half-step. On the guitar, two notes that are one fret apart are separated by a half-step. Two half-steps equals one whole step, which would be two frets distance.

Again, most notes here are one whole-step apart, with the exception being those separated by a half-step.

THE C MAJOR SCALE 25

## HOW TO PLAY THIS SCALE

In Figure 31, start on the 5th string, 3rd fret and place your 2nd finger there. It's indicated by the circle with the "X" through it. This is the root, C.

Play the C, then keeping your 2nd finger there, add your 4th finger at the 5th fret on the same string. Play this note, D.

Now, you can release these notes. On the 4th string at the 2nd fret, place your first finger. Play this E.

Next play F, then G, then on to the 3rd string, similarly. At the end, you'll reach the high C.

The finger you should use for each fret is indicated in Figure 31.

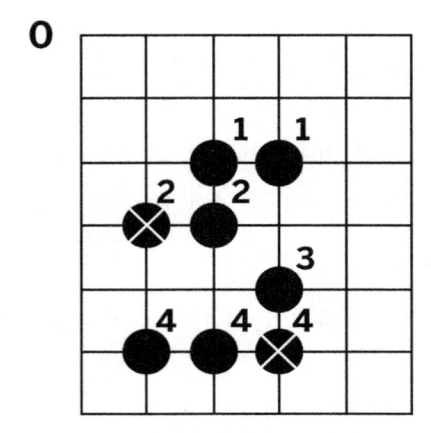

FIG. 31 - C MAJOR SCALE

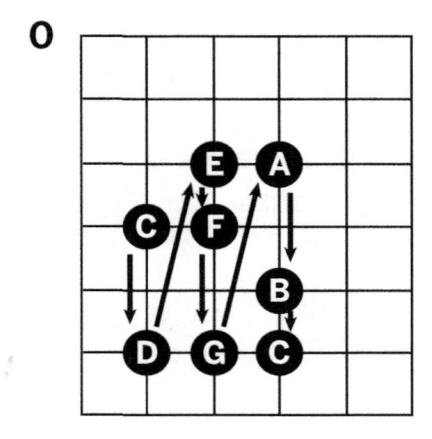

FIG. 32 - C MAJOR SCALE
NOTE NAMES

## MORE ABOUT MAJOR SCALES

A major scale is a series of whole and half-steps.

A half-step is the distance between two notes that are one fret apart. A whole-step is equal to two half-steps.

In all major scales, the half-steps are between the 3rd and 4th notes (or *degrees*) and the 7th and root degrees. All the other notes are a whole step apart, or the equivalent of two frets in distance from each other.

In the C Major scale, the half-steps are between E and F and between B and C. Take note of them in Figure 32.

**26 BEGINNERS GUITAR JUMPSTART: A SEEING MUSIC METHOD BOOK**

# MEMORY SUPERPOWER

To easily remember the fingering of the C Major scale, use this tip:

On the A-string, you use fingers 2 and 4. Next, on the D-string, you use fingers 1, 2 and 4 and on the G-string, you use 1, 3 and 4.

When you say it to yourself a few times, it even starts to sound kind of musical. Say, "2 4, 1 2 4, 1 3 4."

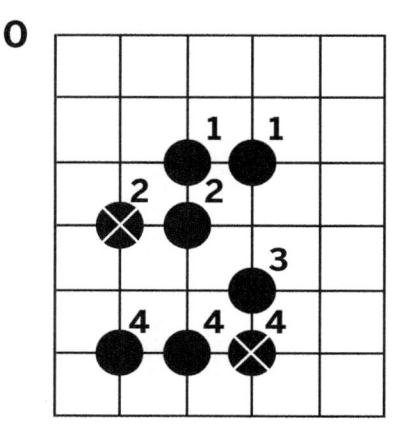

FIG.33 - C MAJOR SCALE

## ASSIGNMENT

### Today's Assignment

Sure, scales help your fingers get used to finding their way around the neck, but aren't they a little boring? No! They will be your superpower, soon letting you access any chord, any melody, anytime.

Play C Major starting with the lowest note (C on the 5th string) and ending with the highest note (C on the 3rd string). Play this a few times until you can make the string changes easily and smoothly.

If you find it difficult to reach all the notes, stop and examine your wrist. Is it bent? It shouldn't be. When your wrist is straight, you'll have the greatest reach possible. Make some adjustments to the angle of your guitar, your wrist, arm and possibly even your guitar height. Review the chapter "Proper Playing Position".

After you successfully can play all 8 notes going up the scale, play them in reverse order, descending down the scale. Start with the top note, C on the 3rd string, and work your way down to C on the 5th string.

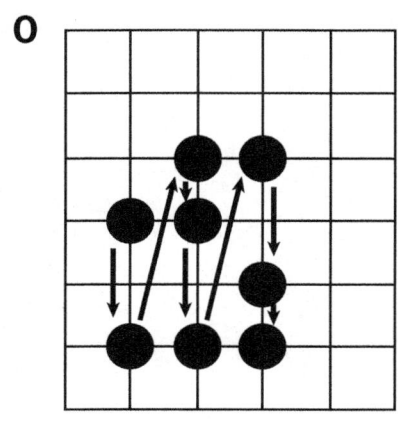

FIG.34 - C MAJOR ASCENDING

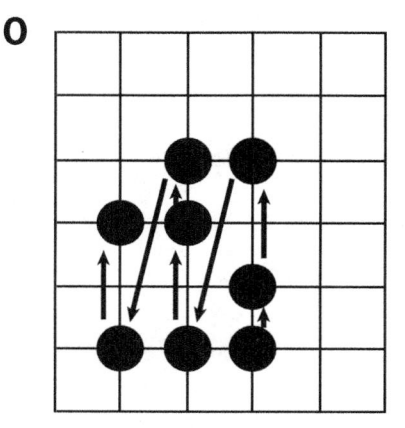

FIG.35 - C MAJOR DESCENDING

**THE C MAJOR SCALE**

28 BEGINNERS GUITAR JUMPSTART: A SEEING MUSIC METHOD BOOK

# DAY 4 - PLAYING YOUR FIRST CHORDS

## MILESTONE

**Play the C Major scale from yesterday.**

**Now, play it again but stop on the 3rd note, E. That E is on the 3rd string, 2nd fret.**

**Take note! That E is in both of the chords you're about to learn.**

## HOW TO PLAY CHORDS

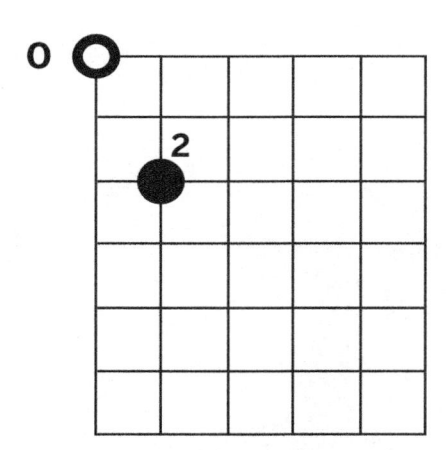

Fig.36 - E5 Chord

Examine the fretboard diagram at left. The numbers indicate which finger to use. Remember, open circles are open strings.

Starting with the 6th string, notice that you will play it open. No fret finger needed.

On the 5th string, place your 2nd finger on the 2nd fret. Keep it there.

Now strum those two strings together with a downward motion as though they were one big note.

Now, try this one based in the key of A. Again, start by noticing that the 6th string has no note, so you'll skip this string.

The 5th string is open. No fret finger required.

On the 4th string, place your 1st finger on the 2nd fret. Keep it there.

Now, strum the 5th and 4th strings together. For a clean sound, avoid hitting the 6th string with your picking hand.

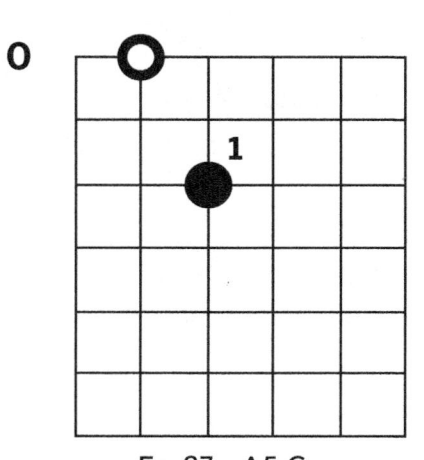

Fig.37 - A5 Chord

Your first two chords! They may be simple chords, but they're chords and you did it! Give yourself a big ol' pat on the back!

## E MAJOR AND A MAJOR CHORDS

E Major and A Major are great pair because they sound great together. That's why they're found in so many songs. Let's build each of these chords, starting with their lowest note.

Starting with the 6th string, notice that you will play it open. No fret finger needed.

On the 5th string, place your 2nd finger on the 2nd fret, just as before.

Now add your 3rd finger to the 4th string, then your 1st finger to the 3rd string. Keep all three fingers there and give a little arch to your hand so it clears the 2nd and 1st strings. Those are open strings and should ring freely.

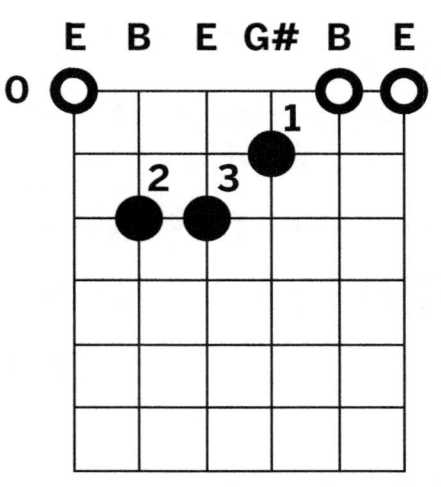

FIG. 38 - E MAJOR CHORD

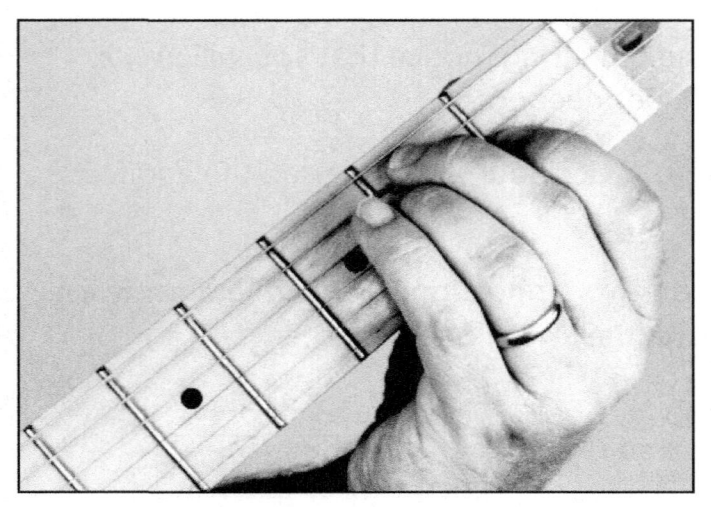

FIG. 39 - E MAJOR HAND POSITION

FIG. 40 - E MAJOR PLAYER'S VIEW

OK, time to strum all 6 strings together. How does it sound? Try it again, strumming each string slowly so you can hear each of the 6 notes. If any sound muffled, make a little adjustment with your hand.

**30 BEGINNERS GUITAR JUMPSTART: A SEEING MUSIC METHOD BOOK**

Chances are, you'll need to make sure your fingers are quite close to the frets and that your hand has enough arch to keep your fingers from accidentally hitting adjacent strings.

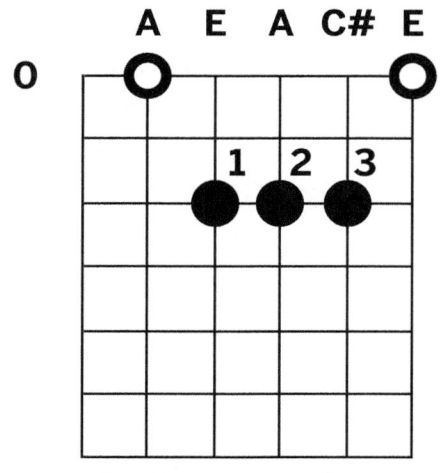

FIG.41 - A MAJOR CHORD

E Major has a big sound because all 6 strings are used. A Major sounds almost as big.

Using the same process, begin at the bottom. Notice that the 6th string is not used, so you'll skip this string.

The 5th string is open. No fret finger required.

On the 4th string, place your 1st finger on the 2nd fret. Keep it there. Add your 2nd finger to the 3rd string, then add your 3rd finger to the 2nd string.

Give a a little arch to your hand so it clears the 1st string. It is open and should ring freely. Give your 5 notes a strum. Again, play each note individually to check out your finger position. If you're doing it right, each note will ring out. If you're not doing it correctly, make some adjustments and try again.

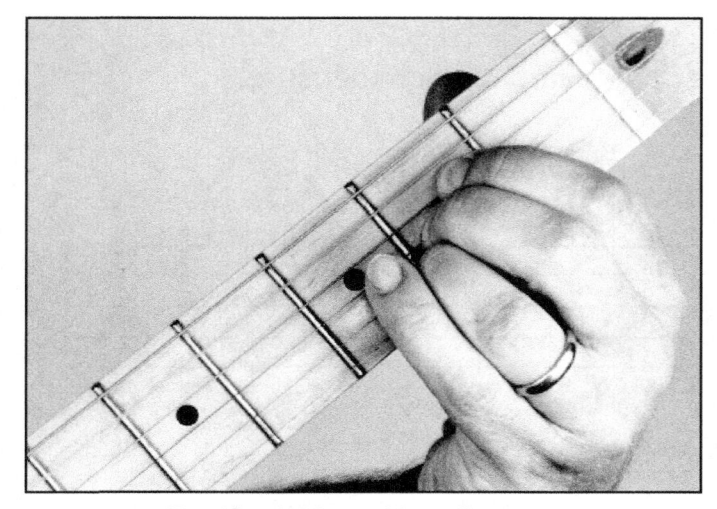

FIG.42 - A MAJOR HAND POSITION

FIG.43 - A MAJOR PLAYER'S VIEW

You did it! Your first two complete chords! This is no small feat and your fingers and brain probably feel a little like spaghetti about now. Every guitarist felt that way when they learned their first chords.

The great news: it gets easier every time you do it.

**PLAYING YOUR FIRST CHORDS**

# SOUNDCHECK

You've already seen quarter-notes. Here is a combination rhythm that uses both quarter-notes and half-notes. A half-note takes the same amount of time as 2 quarter-notes. Out loud, count, "One, Two, Three, Four". Each word is a quarter-note. A half-note would be held for a two-count, like "One, Two" or "Three, Four".

Play these with the simple chords from Figures 36 and 37.

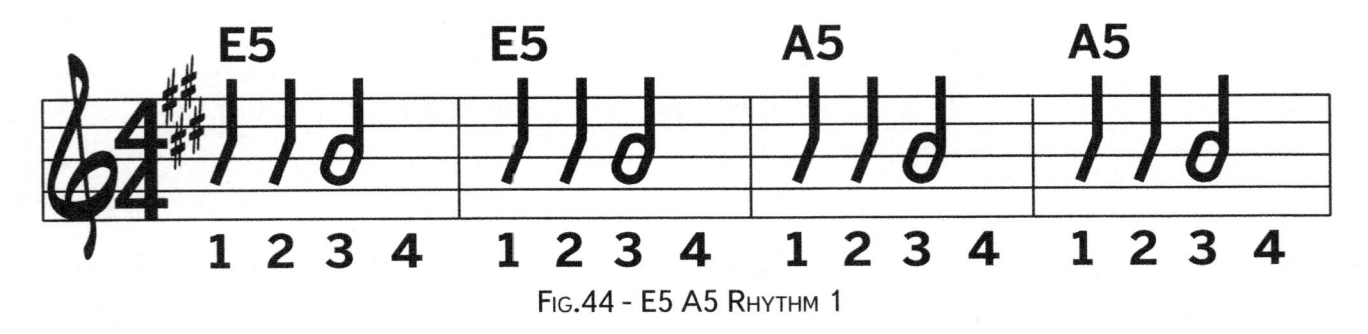

FIG.44 - E5 A5 RHYTHM 1

Here's a variation, with the half-note on the first two beats of each measure.

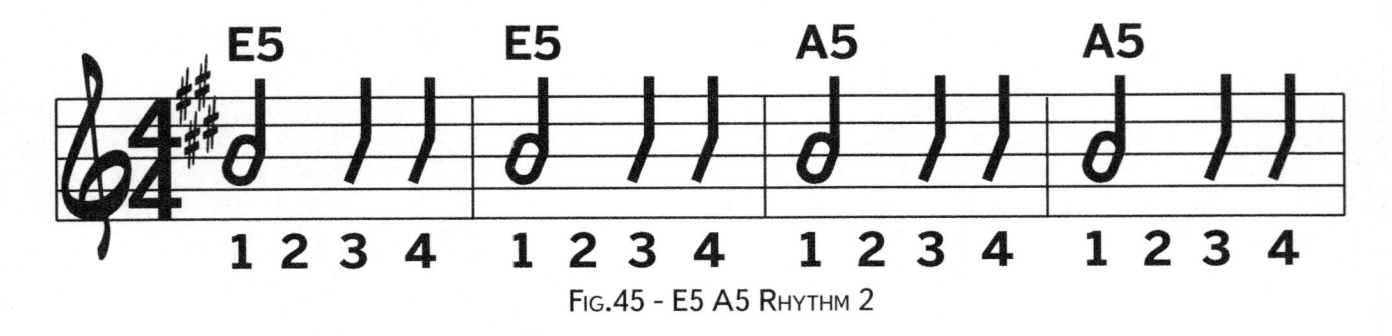

FIG.45 - E5 A5 RHYTHM 2

You know, this is starting to sound a lot like music! Congratulate yourself, musician!

**Today's Assignment**

Try these mini-songs using whole chords, E Major and A Major (Figs 38 and 41). Use a downward motion for each strum.

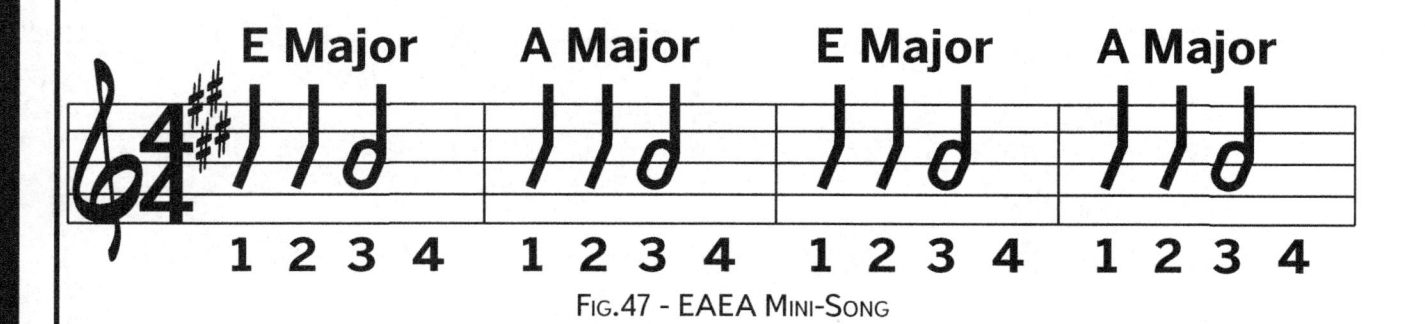

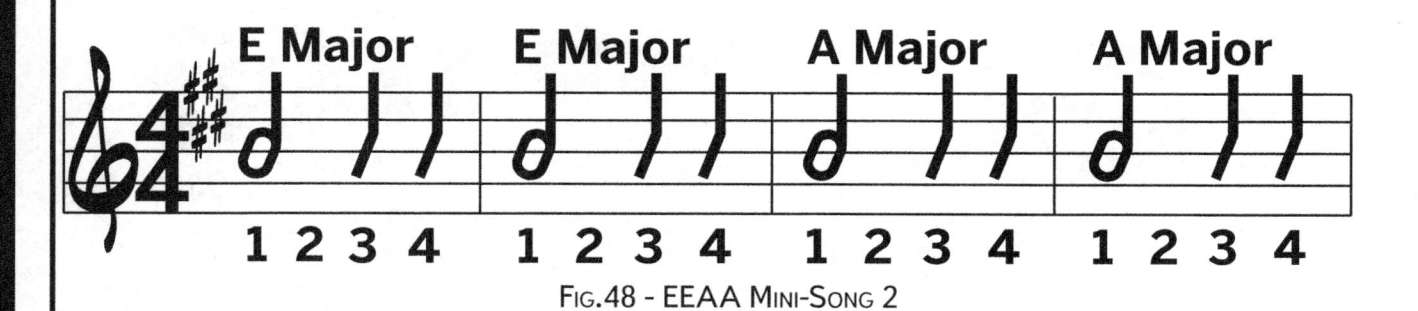

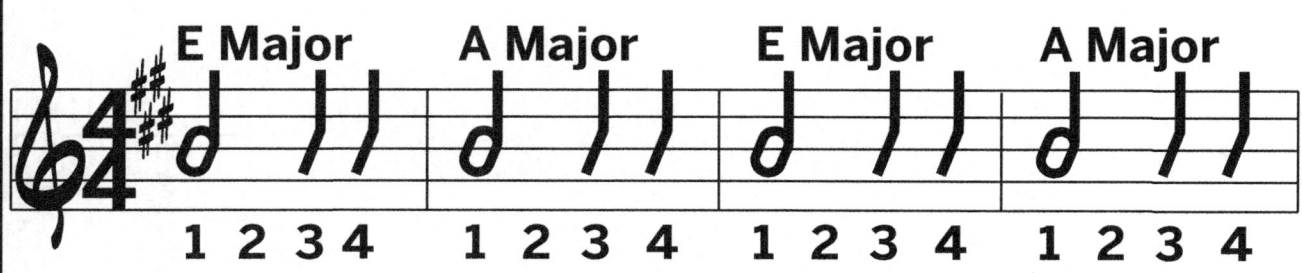

Fig.46 - EEAA Mini-Song

Fig.47 - EAEA Mini-Song

Fig.48 - EEAA Mini-Song 2

Fig.49 - EAEA Mini-Song 2

**PLAYING YOUR FIRST CHORDS**

# Make sure you're learning music the right way from the start.

**Learn Your First Chords Quickly**
**Learn Many Rhythm Patterns**
**Learn Basic Music Concepts and Terms**
**Includes First-Time Ukulele Buyer's Guide**
**Photos of Fingerings from Your Point-of-View**

## SEEING MUSIC METHOD BOOKS

*Learn Basic Lines, Rhythms and Play Your First Songs*

# UKULELE BEGINNERS JUMPSTART
### ANDY SCHNEIDER
BEGINNER

Scan to learn more

See more music.
SeeingMusicBooks.com

**SEEING MUSIC METHOD BOOKS**

**34 BEGINNERS GUITAR JUMPSTART: A SEEING MUSIC METHOD BOOK**

# KNOW YOUR GUITAR

## Acoustic Guitar

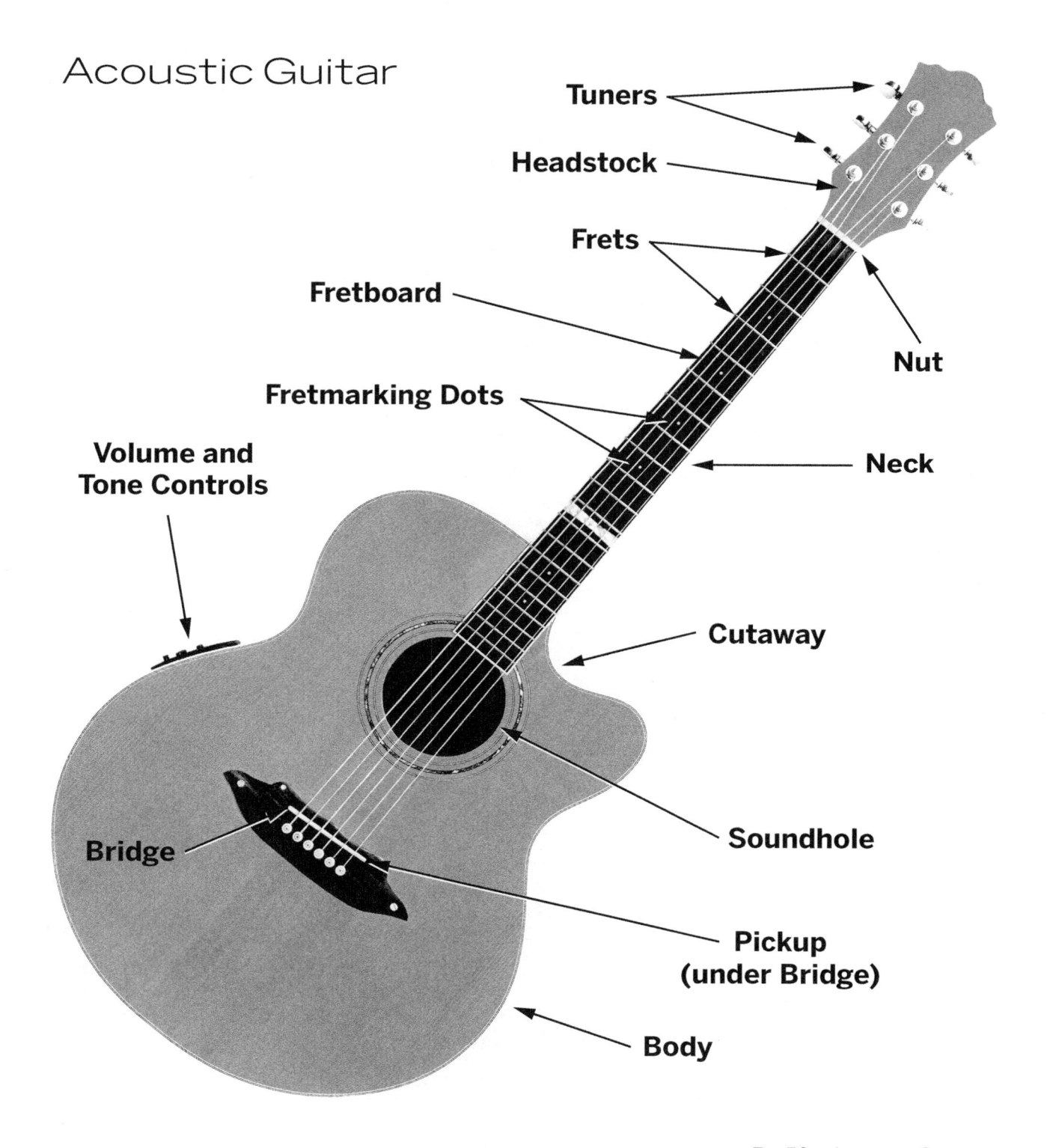

- Tuners
- Headstock
- Frets
- Fretboard
- Nut
- Fretmarking Dots
- Volume and Tone Controls
- Neck
- Cutaway
- Soundhole
- Bridge
- Pickup (under Bridge)
- Body

Fig.50 - Acoustic Guitar

# Electric Guitar

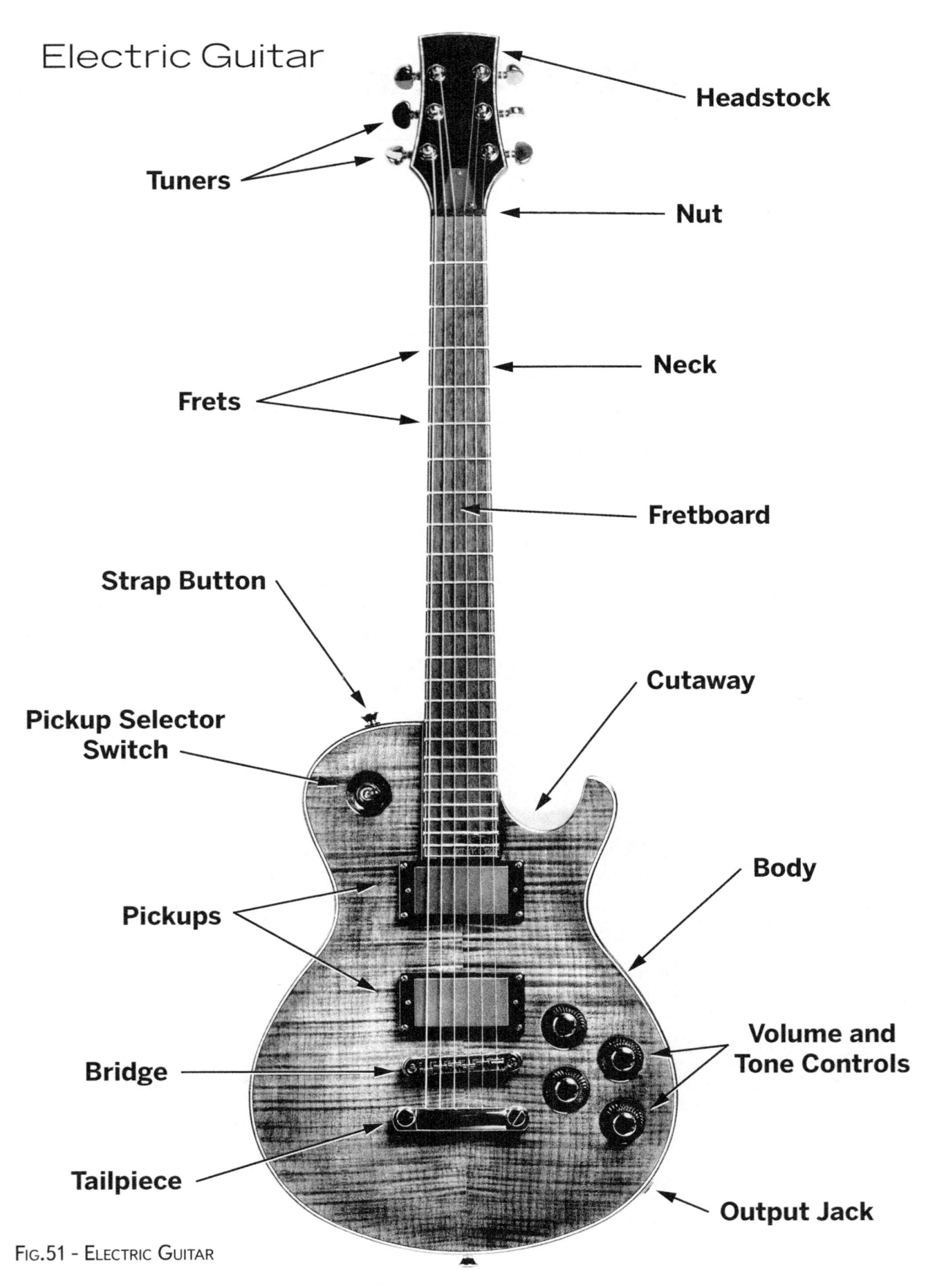

- Headstock
- Tuners
- Nut
- Neck
- Frets
- Fretboard
- Strap Button
- Cutaway
- Pickup Selector Switch
- Body
- Pickups
- Volume and Tone Controls
- Bridge
- Tailpiece
- Output Jack

Fig.51 - Electric Guitar

**36 BEGINNERS GUITAR JUMPSTART: A SEEING MUSIC METHOD BOOK**

# DAY 5 - PLAYING BARRE CHORDS

## MILESTONE

**Play the E Major and A Major chords from yesterday.**

**Those are the full versions of those chords. Would you like to see a little bit easier way to play a A Major?**

## *WHAT ARE BARRE CHORDS?*

A barre chord is a chord where one of your fingers plays more than one string. Examine the fretboard diagrams below. At left, the full version of the A Major chord. At right, the barre chord version.

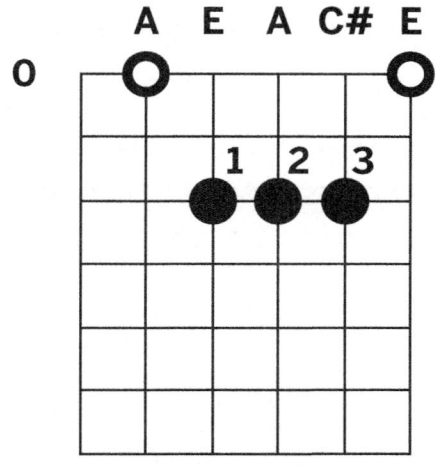

FIG.52 - A MAJOR (FULL VERSION)

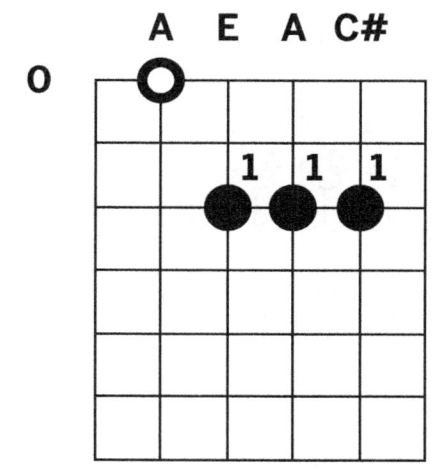

FIG.53 - A MAJOR BARRE

Notice the barre chord version doesn't use the open 1st string. The chord still sounds good and quite full.

Start by placing the tip of your 1st finger on the 4th string at the 2nd fret. Play that note. Now, roll that finger down so it's laying across the next few strings. Just like a log laying across train tracks, you'll use your 1st finger to play all three fretted notes. Try playing those notes. Give a strum to all three, then play each note individually to be sure your fretting hand is positioned well.

Now play all 4 strings of the barre chord. Watch for picking accuracy, being careful to not strum the 1st or 6th strings.

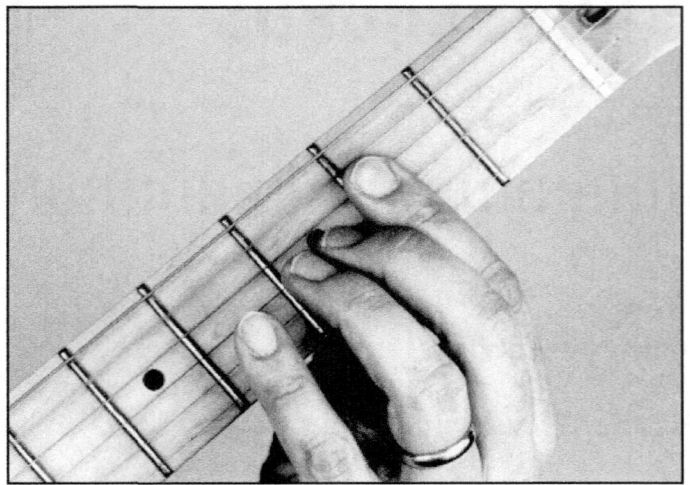

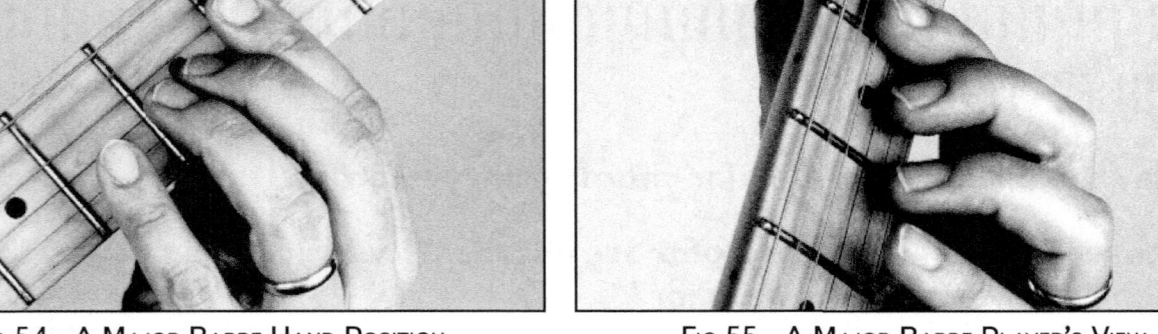

FIG.54 - A MAJOR BARRE HAND POSITION

FIG.55 - A MAJOR BARRE PLAYER'S VIEW

At first, using your finger as a barre may feel awkward. Keep trying it. Your brain will keep tuning the exact position of your fingers until this becomes much easier and sounds great, too.

## B MAJOR BARRE CHORD

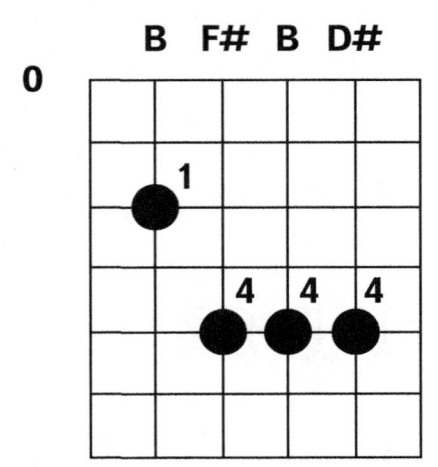

FIG.56 - B MAJOR BARRE

Begin playing this chord with your 1st finger on the 5th string at the 2nd fret. That note is B, the root of the chord. Play that note, just to make sure you're in good position near the fret.

Next, place the tip of your 4th finger on the 4th string at the 4th fret. Play that note. Now, roll that finger down so it's laying across the next few strings.

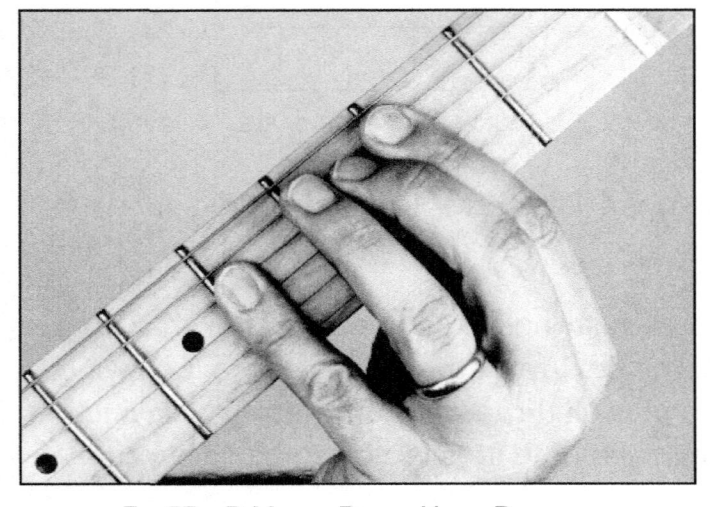

FIG.57 - B MAJOR BARRE HAND POSITION

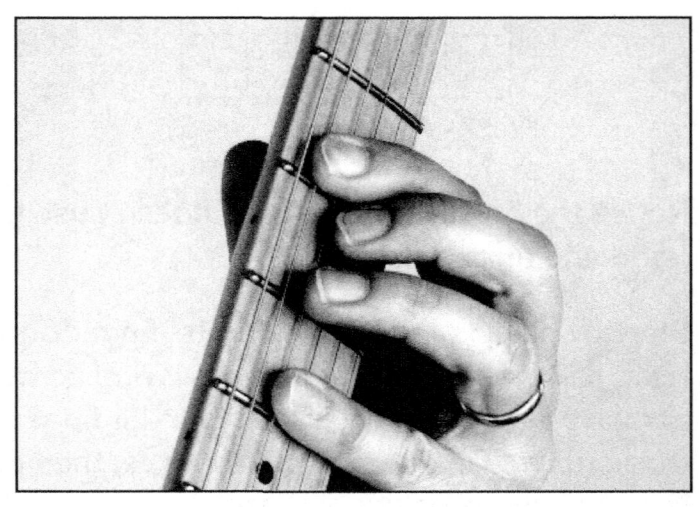

FIG.58 - B MAJOR BARRE PLAYER'S VIEW

# SEEING MUSIC

The title of this book is *Seeing Music*. Do you see the similarity between the A Major barre chord and the B Major barre chord? There are many other barre chords up the neck of the guitar that look just like the B Major barre chord and you're well on your way to knowing all of them!

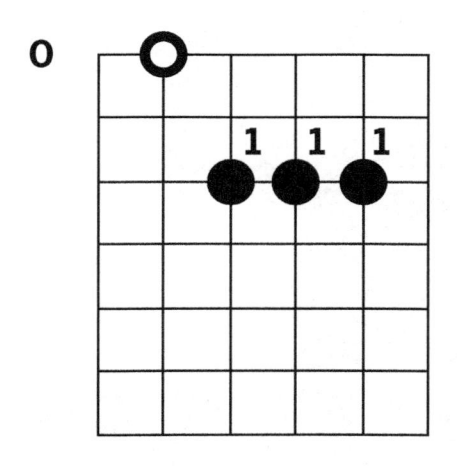

FIG. 59 - A MAJOR BARRE

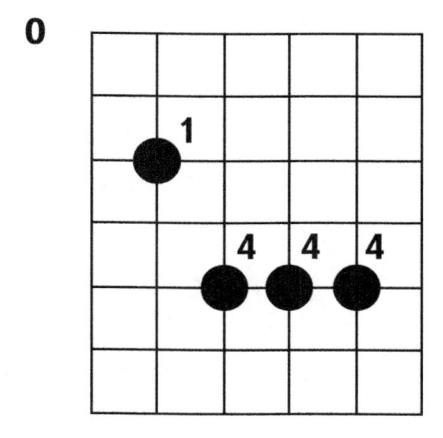

FIG. 60 - B MAJOR BARRE

## Today's Assignment

Try these mini-songs using E, A and B Major chords. These chords sound terrific together and get used in many songs. Use a downward motion for each strum.

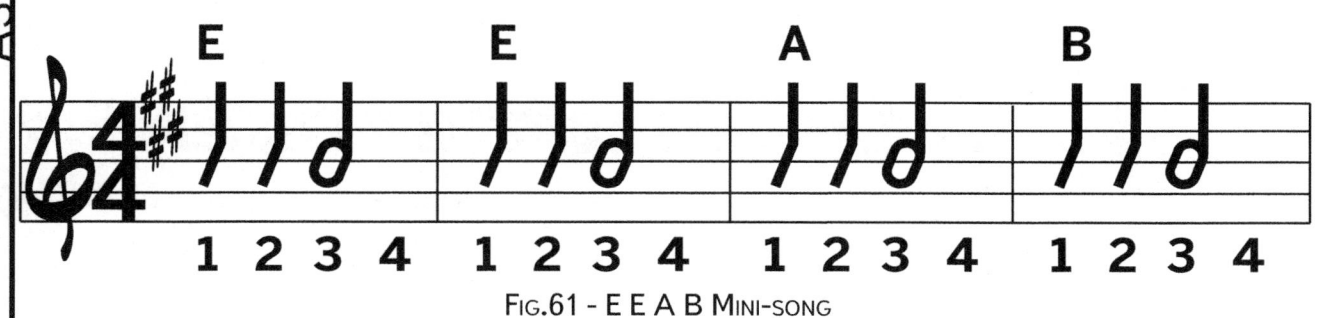

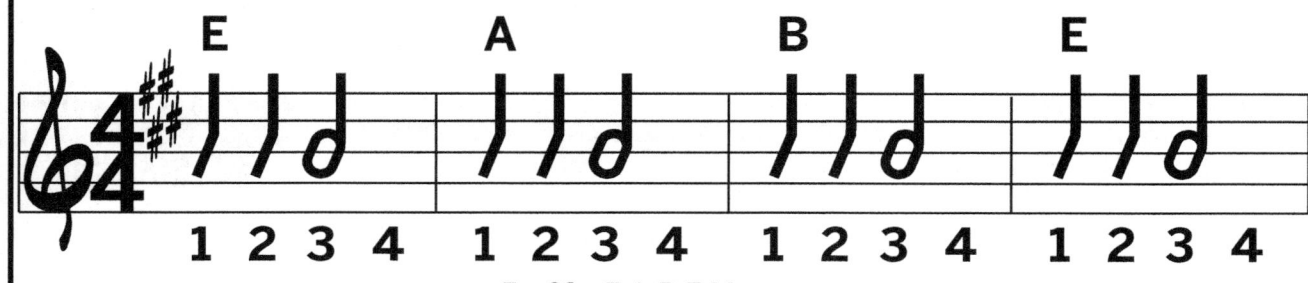

FIG. 61 - E E A B MINI-SONG

FIG. 62 - E A B E MINI-SONG

**PLAYING BARRE CHORDS** 39

# If you can see music, why not listen to this book?

## Listen to This Book!

*Download the free audio examples of these exercises*

Scan and go now

seeingmusicbooks.com

**SEEING MUSIC METHOD BOOKS**

**40 BEGINNERS GUITAR JUMPSTART: A SEEING MUSIC METHOD BOOK**

# KNOW YOUR FRETBOARD (PART I)

One of the most important steps to playing guitar is learning the names of the notes on the fretboard. If you know every note, everything else will be much easier to learn and play. And while the fretboard seems like a huge mess to be memorized, there are some super-easy shortcuts that will make learning much more fun.

## THE FIRST 3 FRETS

Let's consider just the natural notes, those without sharps or flats. Start by playing all of the notes here, one at a time, starting at the bottom.

FIG.63 - FIRST 3 FRET NOTE NAMES

Begin with the open 6th string, noted in the upper-left corner of the diagram. Say the note's name, E as you play the note.

Next, put your 1st finger at first fret of that string, F and say it's name. Then use your 3rd finger to play the third fret, again saying its name, G.

Next, move to the open A string. Keep going, playing B and C, then moving to the 3rd string. Keep ascending that way, moving up the fretboard and across the strings until you get all the way to the high G in the lower right of the figure.

The pitch you hear should get progressively higher with each note.

Note: These notes don't always have to be played with the fingering given here. This is just a good way to begin playing through all the notes.

**BEGINNERS GUITAR JUMPSTART**

# *MEMORIZING THESE EASILY*

Memorizing things can be frustrating. Here's an easy way to remember the locations of the notes in Figure 63.

There really are only three fingerings to remember here. Notice how several of the strings share similar fingerings.

First, notice how the 6th, 2nd and 1st strings, E, B and E, all use the same pattern: open-string, 1st fret and 3rd fret. Memorize this one pattern (open, 1st, 3rd), and you've memorized 3 strings!

Second, notice how the 4th and 5th strings use a slightly different pattern of open-string, 2nd fret and 3rd fret?

The 3rd string, G, is easy to remember because there's only one fretted note to remember, 2nd fret.

**Similar Fingerings**

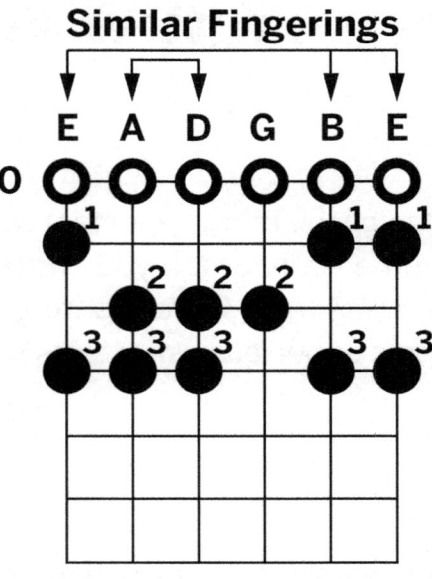

FIG.64 - FIRST 3 FRET FINGERINGS

# SEEING MUSIC

Do you see how the notes of the B string and both E strings can be played with similar fingerings?

Do you see how the notes of the A and D strings are also similarly fingered?

### Today's Assignment

Play all the natural notes from the exercise above in ascending order, saying the note names as you go.

Once you get those memorized, challenge yourself by playing them in descending order.

# DAY 6 - G AND C MAJOR

## MILESTONE

**Play the C Major scale from earlier.**

**Scales types (like the major scale) are defined by their combination of whole and half-steps and the note they start on (the root).**

**Let's start a major scale on a different note, G.**

## *HOW TO PLAY A G MAJOR SCALE*

Below are the scales for C Major and G Major. Notice how they look very similar? That's because they both use the same combination of whole and half-steps. That's not surprising because ALL major scales use the same combination of whole and half-steps.

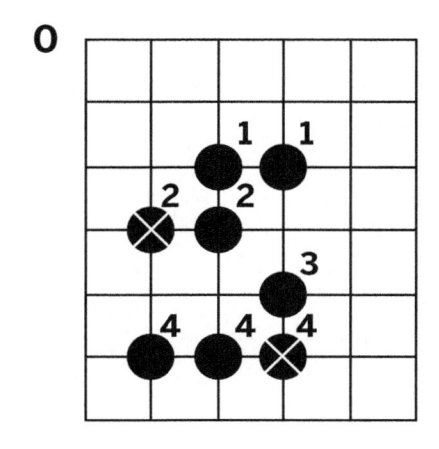

FIG.65 - C MAJOR SCALE

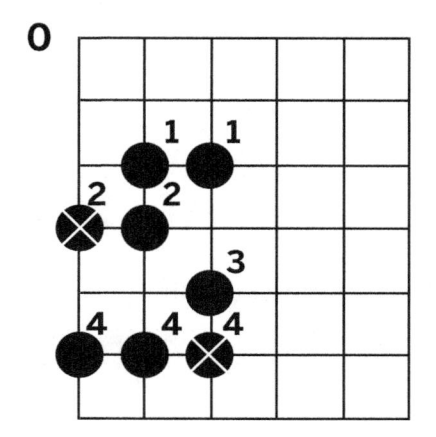

FIG.66 - G MAJOR SCALE

Just as you did with C Major, start with your 2nd finger. This time place it on the 6th string at the 3rd fret. Follow the diagram, playing the ascending scale.

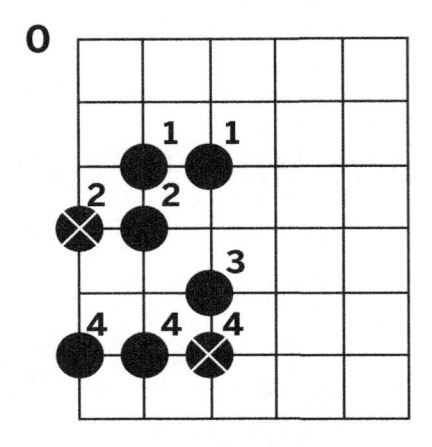

Fig. 67 - G Major Scale

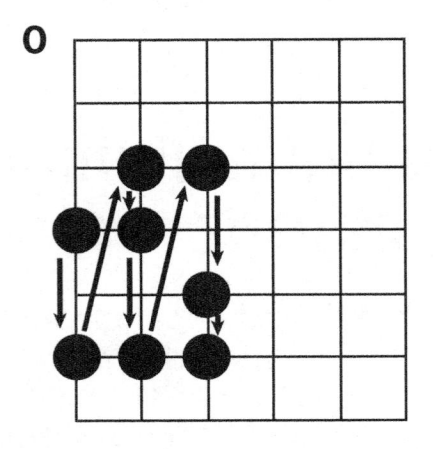

Fig. 68 - G Major Scale

Here are the note names of the scale you just played.

# GABCDEF#G

Fig. 69 - G Major Note Names

See how the half-steps are between the 3rd and 4th, 7th and root degrees of the scale? This is just the same in the C Major scale and every other major scale.

See the symbol by F, the 7th degree? That is a sharp symbol. That means that it is one half-step higher than F natural.

## ALL ABOUT SHARPS AND FLATS

When a note is raised a half-step, we say it is *sharp*. When a note is lowered a half-step, we say it is *flat*. When it is neither, we say it is *natural*.

Here are three notes, C, C# and D. Because C sharp is also one half-step below D, we could also call it by another name: D flat. D flat and C sharp are the same note.

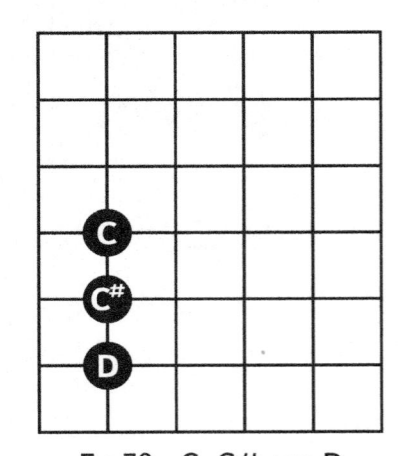

Fig. 70 - C, C# and D

Similarly, here are F, F# and G. We could call the middle note either F sharp or G flat.

It's OK to describe a note by its natural name, such as *F natural* and *G natural*. However, for the sake of convenience, we generally just say "F" and "G".

## PLAYING G AND C MAJOR CHORDS

Let's take a look at two more common chords that sound great together. We'll again build our chords by starting from the bottom of the chord, the lowest note.

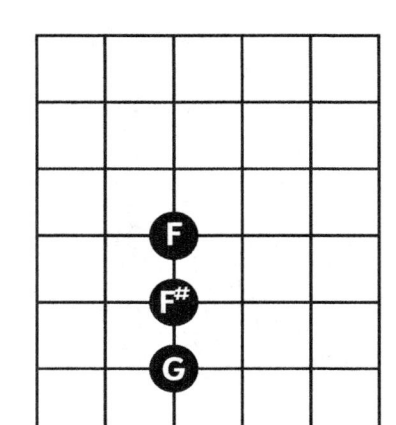

FIG.71 - F, F# AND G

Place your 2nd finger on the 6th string, 3rd fret. This is the root, G.

Add your 1st finger to the 5th string, 2nd fret.

Now, the next few strings are played open, so you'll need to give a little clearance between the strings and your palm.

Using your 4th finger, fret the 1st string at the 3rd fret. Now, give it a strum.

Play each note of the chord slowly, to be sure it is ringing well. If not, make an adjustment with your fretting hand.

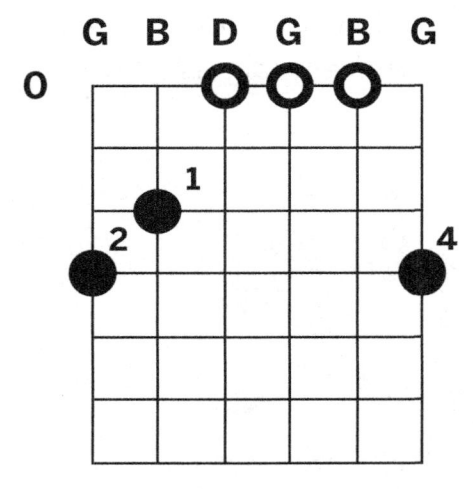

FIG.72 - G MAJOR CHORD

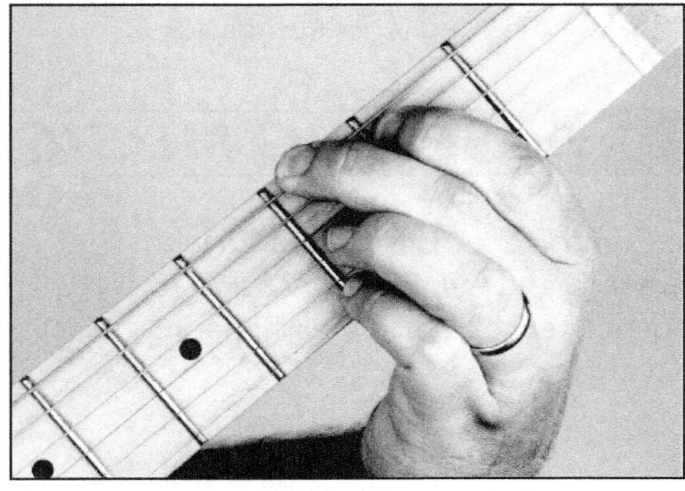

FIG.73 - G MAJOR HAND POSITION

FIG.74 - G MAJOR PLAYER'S VIEW

Now, let's try C Major. Again, build from the bottom.

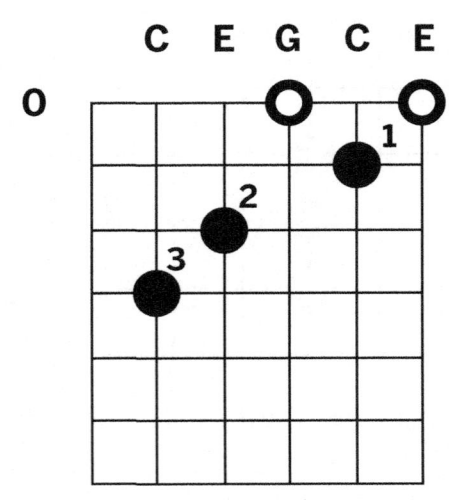

FIG.75 - C MAJOR CHORD

Start with your 3rd finger on the 5th string at the 3rd fret. This is the root, C.

Add your 2nd finger to the 4th string at the 2nd fret.

The 3rd string is played open, no fretting required.

Add your 1st finger to the 2nd string at the 1st fret.

The 1st string is open, no fretting required.

Keep in mind, the 6th string isn't used here, so avoid picking it. Give your C Major chord a strum. Just as with G Major, you'll need to clear the open strings.

If you have trouble with either of these chords, getting the open strings to ring well, chances are your fingers could be more upright at the fingertips. Don't let your fingers become lazy and sag toward the fretboard. They will need to stand with precision over the strings.

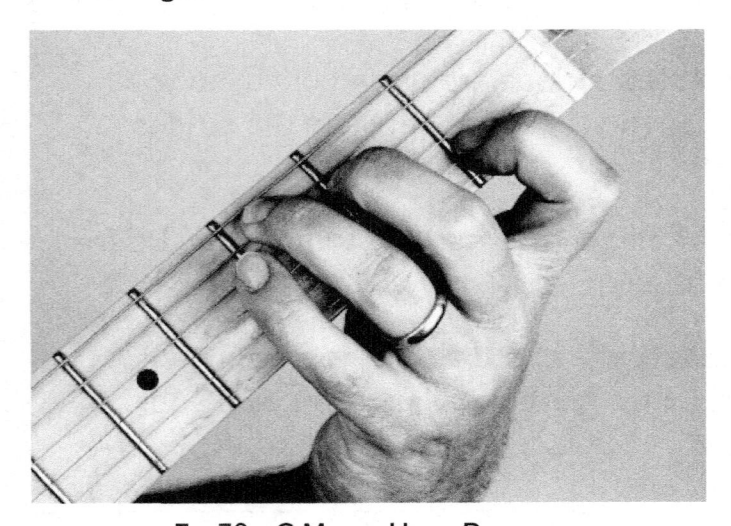

FIG.76 - C MAJOR HAND POSITION

FIG.77 - C MAJOR PLAYER'S VIEW

# SEEING MUSIC

Notice how different the appearance of the G and C chords is compared with E, A and B. Now look for the similarity between G and C in Figures 72 and 75. Notice the diagonal slope of the lowest 3 notes of each? While their fingering is quite different, their shapes are somewhat similar.

**46 BEGINNERS GUITAR JUMPSTART: A SEEING MUSIC METHOD BOOK**

## Today's Assignment

Here are a couple chord progressions using G and C chords.

In these charts, play the chord indicated four times, once for each hash mark. Watch out for the order of the chords and the changing rhythms! Each one is a little different.

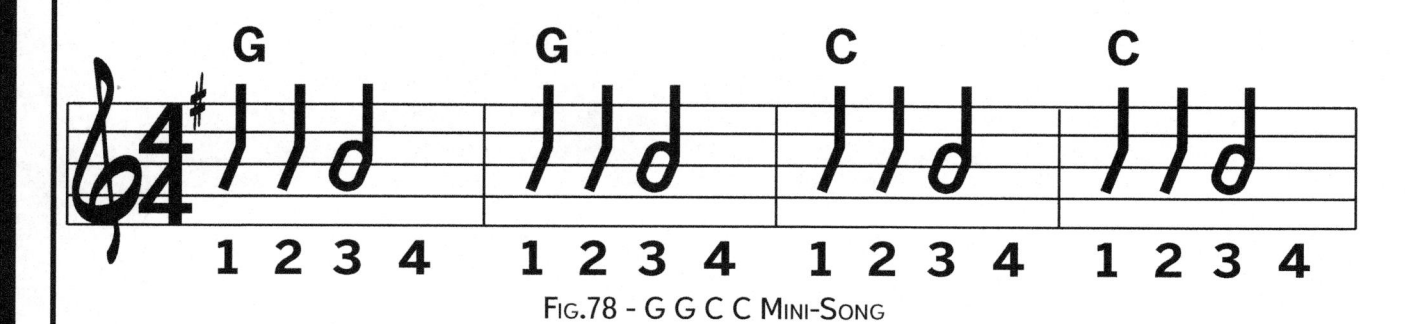

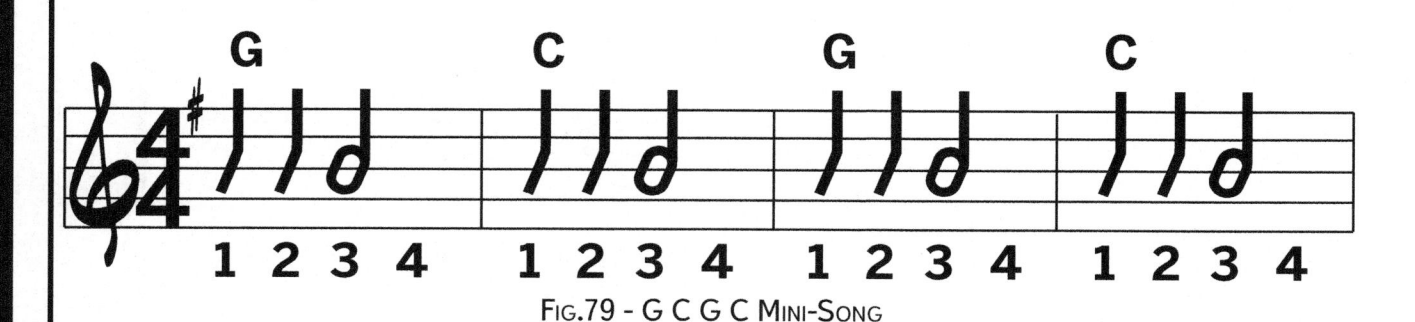

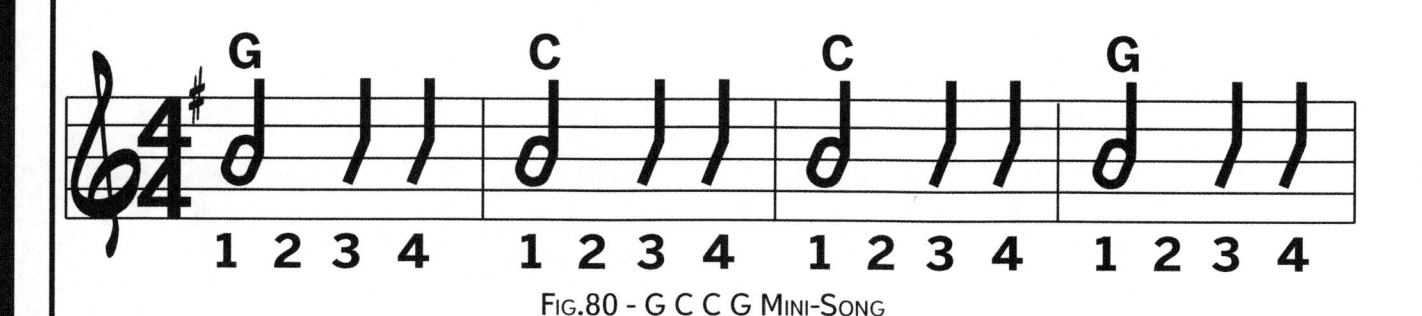

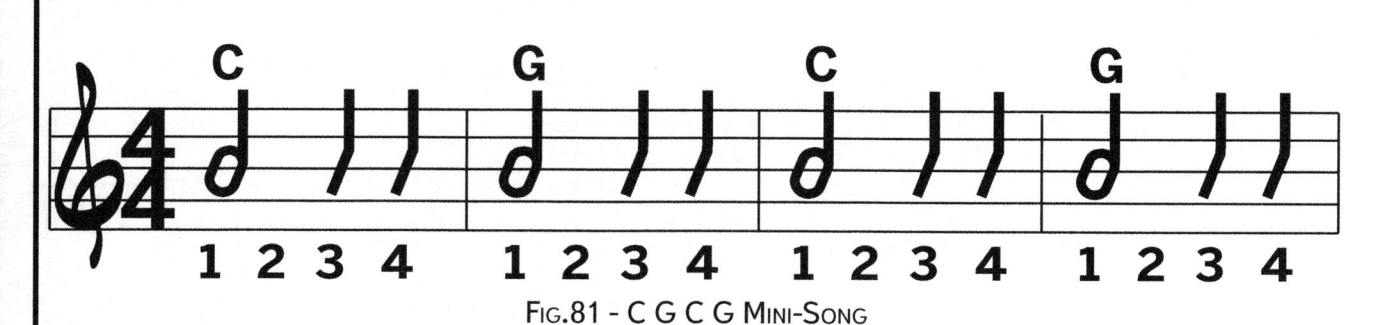

Fig. 78 - G G C C Mini-Song

Fig. 79 - G C G C Mini-Song

Fig. 80 - G C C G Mini-Song

Fig. 81 - C G C G Mini-Song

48 BEGINNERS GUITAR JUMPSTART: A SEEING MUSIC METHOD BOOK

# DAY 7 - THE D MAJOR CHORD

## MILESTONE

**Play the E Major and A Major chords from yesterday. Play the B Major barre chord, then the E Major again.**

**See how those three chords sound like a set that goes together?**

**Now, play G Major and C Major. There is a third chord that completes their set as well. It is D Major.**

## *HOW TO PLAY D MAJOR*

Have a look at the D Major chord below. Notice how its lowest note is on the 4th string. It is the open D string and D is the root of the chord.

Start by placing your 1st finger on the 3rd string at the 2nd fret. Add your 3rd finger to the 2nd string at the 3rd fret.

Finally, add your 2nd finger to the 1st string at the 2nd fret.

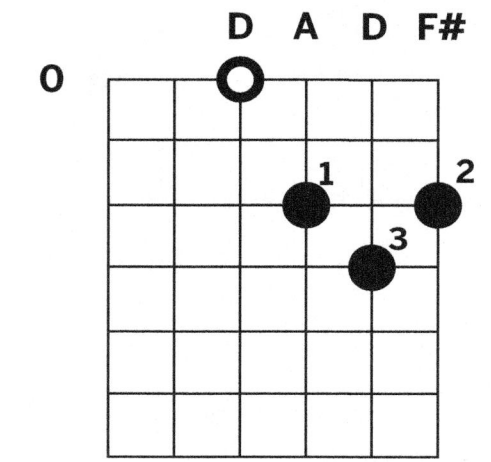

FIG.82 - D MAJOR CHORD

Give it a strum, avoiding picking the 6th and 5th strings. Isn't that a pretty chord!

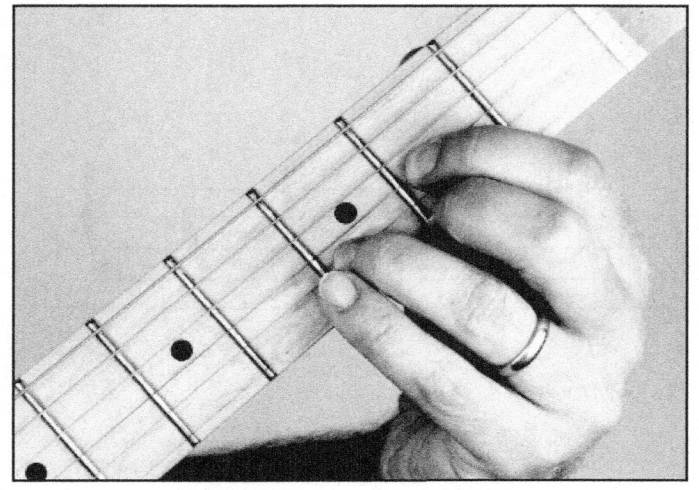

FIG.83 - D MAJOR HAND POSITION

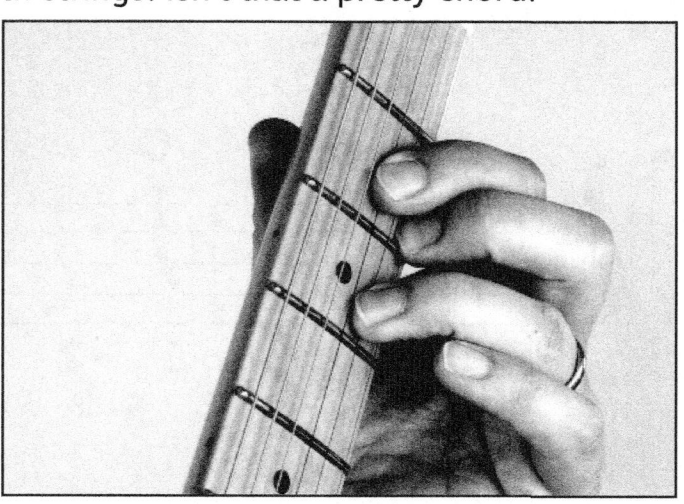

FIG.84 - D MAJOR PLAYER'S VIEW

## 3/4 TIME SIGNATURE

You know that many songs are in 4/4 time. This means there are four quarter-notes per measure. Another time signature is 3/4 (pronounced *three-four*).

3/4 time has three quarter notes per measure. Every waltz is in 3/4 time. That's what makes it a waltz.

## SOUNDCHECK

Let's play a simple waltz using G, C and D Major.

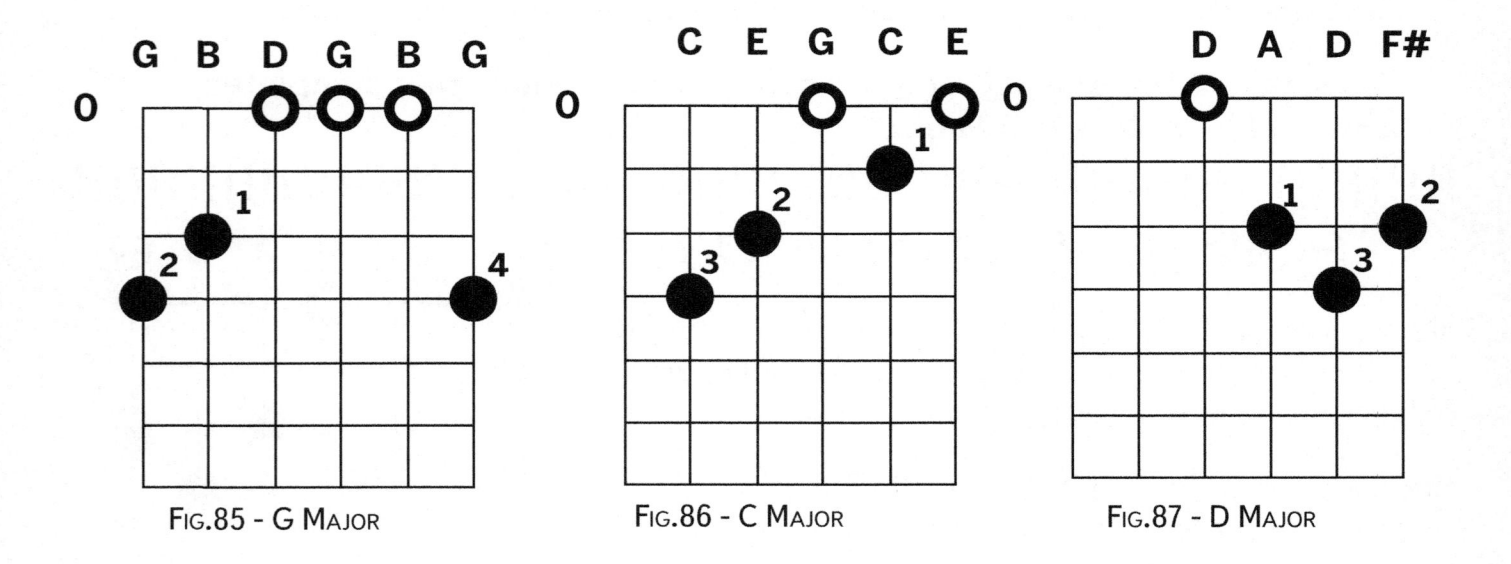

FIG.85 - G MAJOR

FIG.86 - C MAJOR

FIG.87 - D MAJOR

Refer to the chords above for fingerings. Play each chord with a downstroke, three times per measure.

Keep time smoothly and work to make the transitions from chord to chord smooth and seamless.

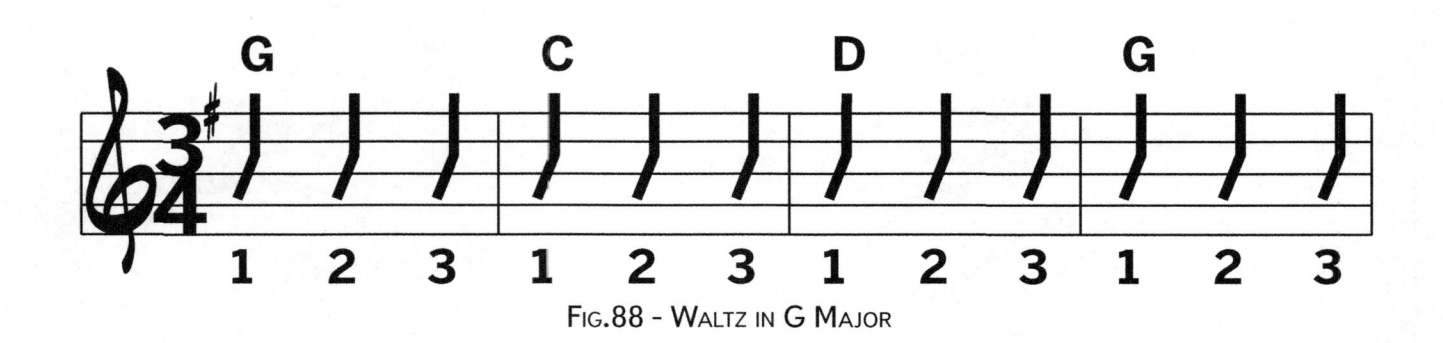

FIG.88 - WALTZ IN G MAJOR

**50 BEGINNERS GUITAR JUMPSTART: A SEEING MUSIC METHOD BOOK**

**Today's Assignment**

Here are a variety of mini-songs using G, C and D chords. Many measures use two chords per bar so you'll be changing fingering more frequently. Use a downward motion for each strum.

Notice Figures 91 and 92 are in 3/4 time!

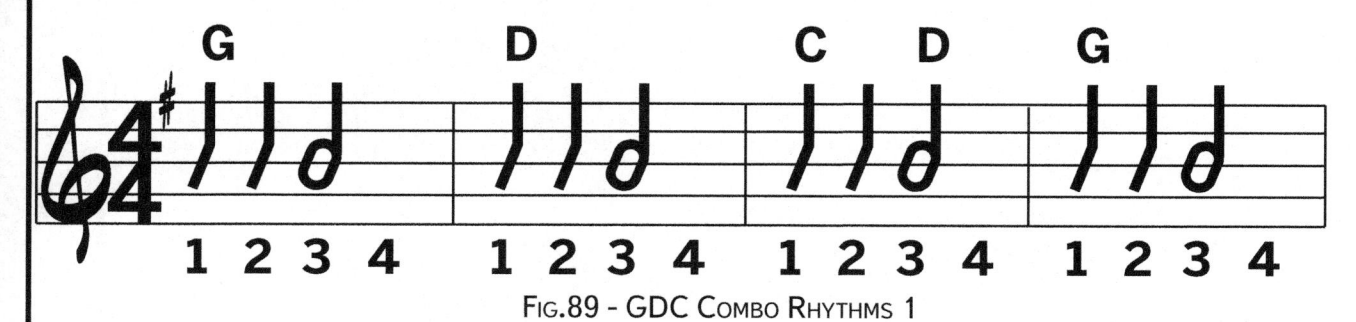

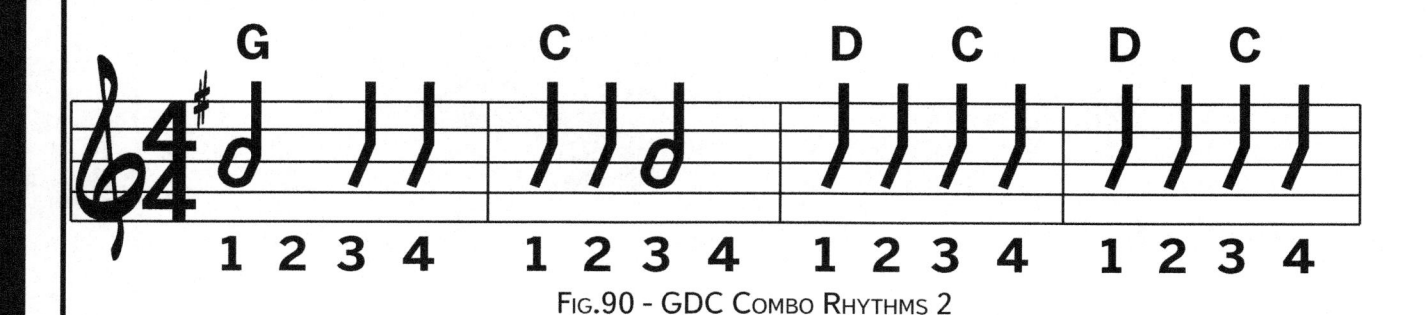

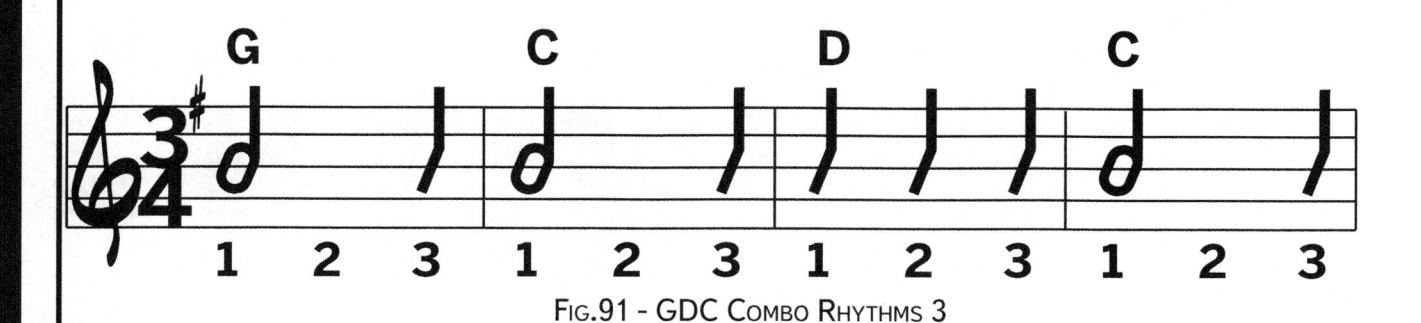

FIG. 89 - GDC Combo Rhythms 1

FIG. 90 - GDC Combo Rhythms 2

FIG. 91 - GDC Combo Rhythms 3

FIG. 92 - GDC Combo Rhythms 4

**THE D MAJOR CHORD 51**

**Infinity is waiting for you.**

## GUITAR SCALES INFINITY

**SEEING MUSIC METHOD BOOKS**

- Utilize Scales and Modes Common to Genres
- Apply Major and Minor Pentatonics Creatively
- Learn the Shortcuts to Memorizing Scales
- Includes Scale/Chord/Genre Styleguide
- Apply Scales with Loads of Exercises

*Master the Universe of Scales in Every Style and Genre*

**ANDY SCHNEIDER**

**INTERMEDIATE TO ADVANCED**

Scan to learn more

See more music.
SeeingMusicBooks.com

**SEEING MUSIC METHOD BOOKS**

52 BEGINNERS GUITAR JUMPSTART: A SEEING MUSIC METHOD BOOK

# DAY 8 - NEW STRUMMING PATTERNS

Music is made of three elements: melody, harmony and rhythm. Melody is the singable part, generally a single note line. Harmony is all the other notes going on simultaneously that support the melody. Both melodies and harmonies have rhythm, and good rhythm helps keep things interesting.

## *WHAT GOES DOWN MUST COME UP*

Strumming is made of two parts: the downstroke and the upstroke. Every downstroke must have an upstroke. Otherwise, your picking hand would go down toward the floor and never return, right? The upstroke brings your hand back to its starting position.

Down, up, down, up. That's what we'll work on now, because that motion is the basis for all good rhythm.

FIG. 93 - DOWNSTROKE

FIG. 94 - UPSTROKE

Work on this motion silently, at first. Following the down and upstroke symbols, move your strumming hand over the strings without actually touching any of them. This is just to get a feel for the motion.

FIG. 95 - EIGHTH-NOTES

The rhythmic motion you're playing are eighth-notes. Just as you'd imagine, two eighth-notes equal one quarter-note. The rhythm is counted, "One-and-Two-and-Three-and-Four-and".

Now, place your left hand to fret an E Major chord. Try the same eighth-note strum. Down, then up and repeat.

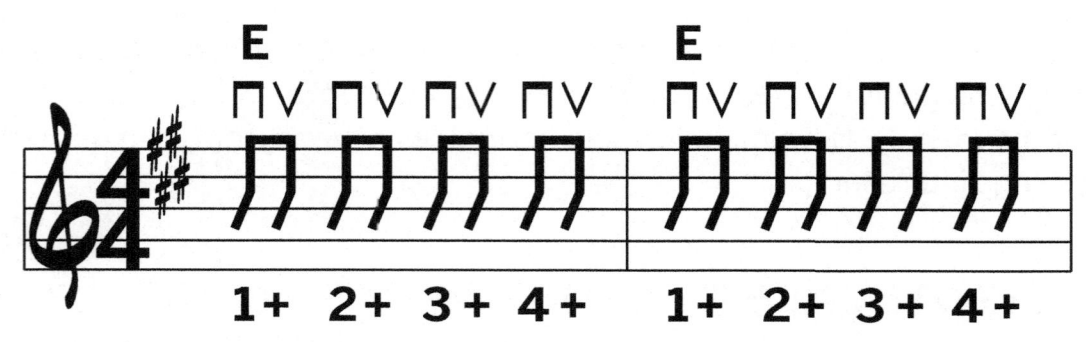

FIG.96 - UP AND DOWNSTROKES

## HOW TO ADD UPSTROKES

Here's the basic downstroke pattern you've been using until now. Try it again, this time taking note of how often your hand silently makes the upstroke. A silent stroke is called a *reststroke*.

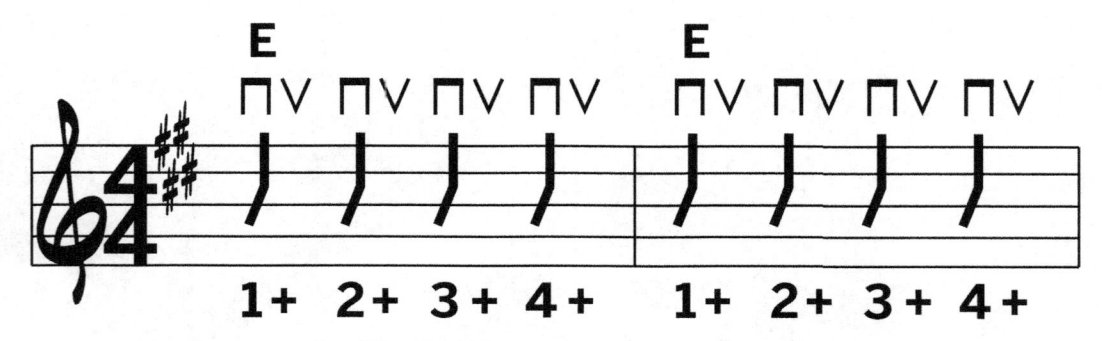

FIG.97 - DOWNSTROKES WITH RESTSTROKES

Instead of just four strokes, you were really making eight: four downward and against the strings and four silent upstrokes!

Ordinarily, downstroke and upstroke marks are only shown for the chords you should play. The reststrokes are not usually indicated.

This is a combination rhythm. Your picking hand will continue the down, up, down, up steady movement. Just as before, sometimes you'll use silent upstrokes (reststrokes) and sometimes you'll strum the strings on the upstrokes.

FIG.98 - COMBINATION DOWN, UP, RESTSTROKES

Here's a different combination of silent and sounded upstrokes.

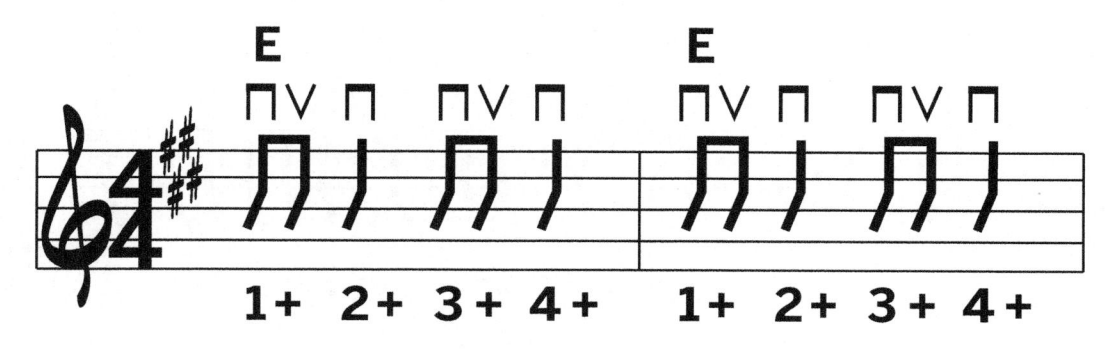

FIG.99 - COMBO 2

This is a very common rhythm used in thousands of songs.

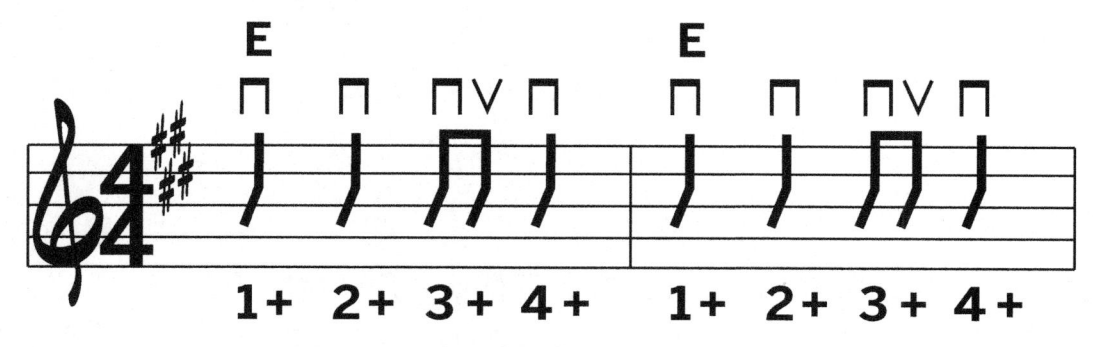

FIG.100 - COMBO 3

**NEW STRUMMING PATTERNS**

## Today's Assignment

You've been playing combination rhythms using quarter- and eighth-notes. These combinations make music fantastic and much more interesting.

Start the following chord progressions slowly at first. The goal is very steady rhythm and smooth transitions between chords.

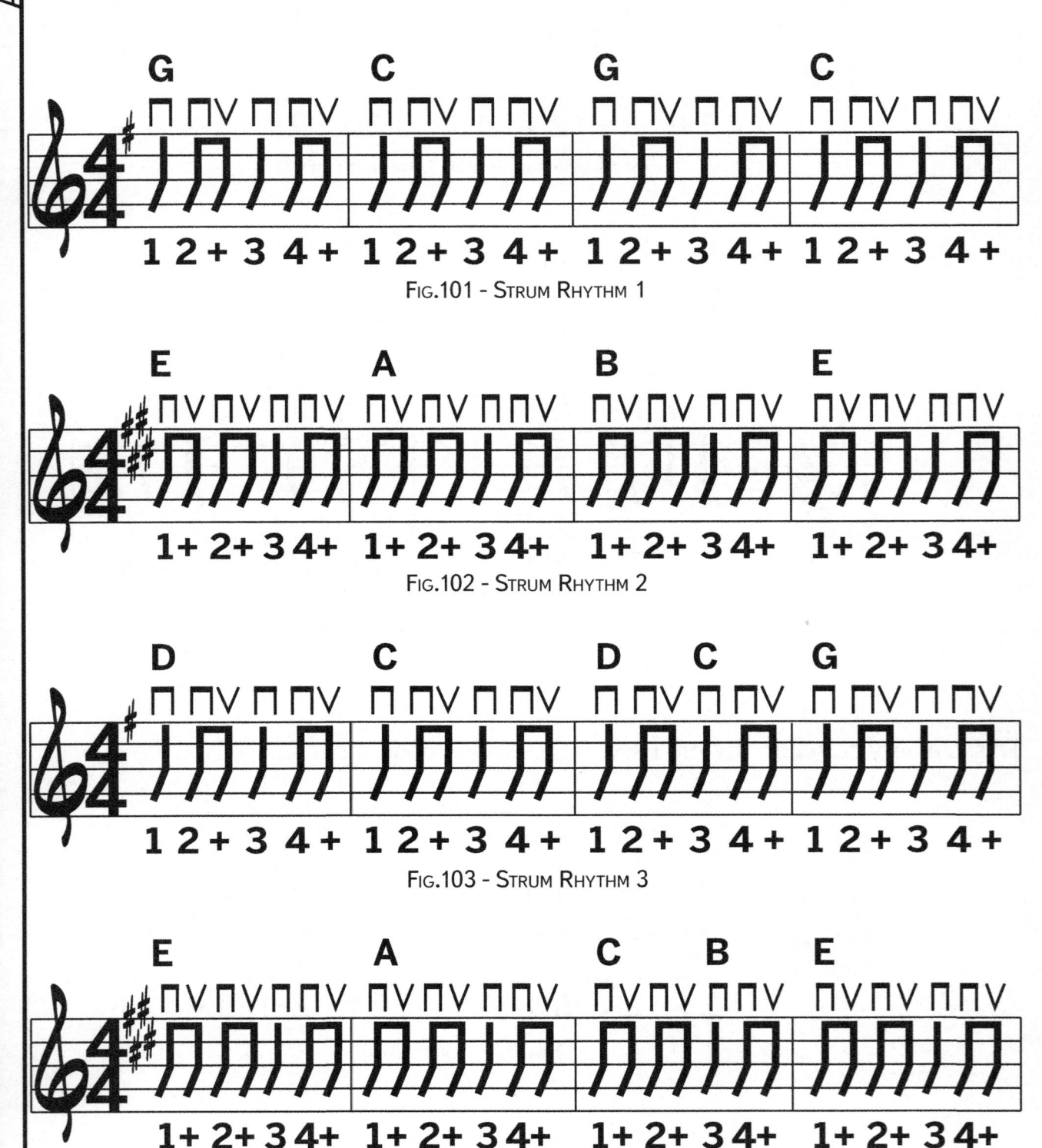

FIG.101 - STRUM RHYTHM 1

FIG.102 - STRUM RHYTHM 2

FIG.103 - STRUM RHYTHM 3

FIG.104 - STRUM RHYTHM 4

# KNOW YOUR FRETBOARD (PART II)

You've already learned the names of the natural notes up to the 3rd fret. Let's take a look at a very special fret, the 5th fret.

## *THE FIFTH FRET*

Remember the first three natural notes on the 6th string? They are E, F and G. Want to guess what the next one is?

It's A and it's found at the 5th fret.

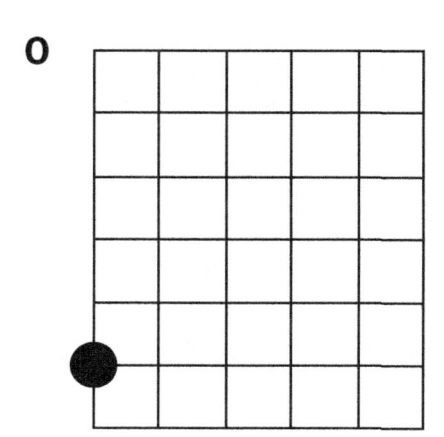

FIG.105 - 6TH STRING 5TH FRET A

What's the name of your 5th string? It's A as well, right? Well, these are the same note, played two different ways.

Play both these notes to confirm they are the same pitch.

Sometimes in guitar playing, it's really convenient to have a couple of options for a given note. Many notes exist in several places around the neck.

Let's look at some more you already know.

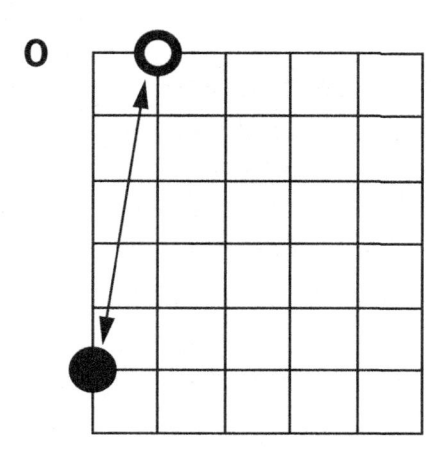

FIG.106 - SAME NOTE ON TWO STRINGS

Three of these equivalent notes are in the C Major scale. Start playing the C Major scale. The first note is C. The second note is D. Stop! You're playing the note D on the 5th string at the 5th fret. What's the name of the 4th string? It's D! Confirm they're the same note by playing both the 5th string, 5th fret D and the open 4th string D.

Pretty neat, right? Figure 108 shows these open-string equivalent notes.

FIG.107 - C MAJOR SCALE

Keep going, you know more than that! Again, let's start playing the C Major scale. C, D, E, F, G..Stop. You should be on the 4th string at the 5th fret. You've probably already guessed: This G is the same as the open 3rd string G.

One more: Starting at the bottom, C, D, E, F, G, A, B..Stop! Now you're on the 3rd string at the 4th fret. This is the same B as the open 2nd string B. But wait, all the other note equivalents were at the 5th fret. What's up, here?

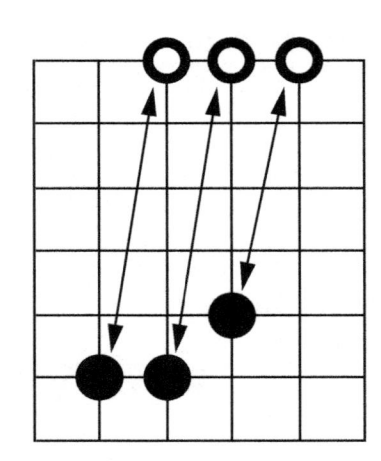

FIG.108 - OPEN STRING EQUIVALENTS

## THE EVIL B STRING

OK, it's not really evil. But, its unusual tuning does complicate guitar players lives quite a bit. It also is what makes guitar harmonies beautiful. Have a look.

The pitch distance between the 3rd and 2nd strings, G and B, is unique. All the other strings are spaced the same interval apart. This makes learning the guitar slightly tricky, especially when it comes to making this jump across the G and B strings. It's also what gives the guitar its magic — the ability to make so many beautiful chords. And while it takes time to appreciate, know that the guitar is tuned as it is for a reason. A really great reason.

There's only one more equivalent here. Play the 2nd string at the 5th fret. This note is E and it's the same E as the open 1st string. Check it out.

Here is a diagram of the equivalent pitches of the open strings.

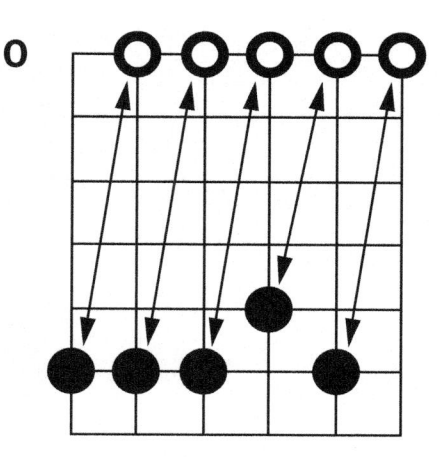

FIG.109 - OPEN STRING EQUIVALENTS

# SOUNDCHECK

The natural notes of the first three frets can easily be remembered by grouping them with other strings that use a similar fingering (see chapter "Know Your Fretboard - Part I").

Many notes on the guitar can be found in several places on the fretboard.

The open-strings have equivalents, generally at the 5th fret. The exception is the 2nd string, open B, whose equivalent note is found at the 4th fret of the 3rd string.

Strings are generally tuned the same interval apart, the exception being the 2nd and 3rd strings.

## Today's Assignment

Review the notes through the 5th fret, starting with the open 6th string, E. Work your way up the natural notes to the 5th fret, saying the names as you go. Take note of the open-string equivalents.

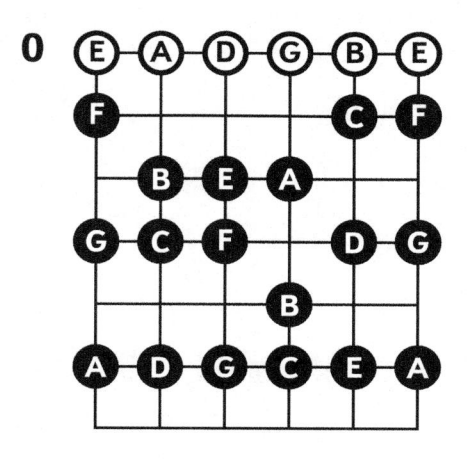

FIG.110 - NATURAL NOTES

**KNOW YOUR FRETBOARD - PART TWO**

**A Complete Method for Classroom.
Learning together. The fun and easy way.**

Teach Their First Chords Quickly

# SEEING MUSIC
## METHOD BOOKS

- Learn Your First Chords Quickly
- Strum Many Favorite and Classic Songs
- Learn Basic Music Concepts and Terms
- Learn the Guitar's Anatomy and Basic Care
- Learn Many Strumming Patterns

Student's Edition - Learn Basic Chords, Rhythms and Strumming

Instructor's Edition - Teach Basic Chords, Rhythms and Strumming

# GUITAR FOR THE CLASSROOM
**ANDY SCHNEIDER**
BEGINNER

Scan to learn more

See more music at SeeingMusicBooks.com

**SEEING MUSIC METHOD BOOKS**

**60 BEGINNERS GUITAR JUMPSTART: A SEEING MUSIC METHOD BOOK**

# DAY 9 - MINOR CHORDS

||||||||||||||||||||||||||||||||||||||||||||||||||||||||||||||||||||||||||||||||||

## MILESTONE

**Play the E Major and A Major chords.**

**Every chord has a major version and a minor version.**

||||||||||||||||||||||||||||||||||||||||||||||||||||||||||||||||||||||||||||||||||

## *HOW TO PLAY E MINOR*

Look at the two chords below. You're familiar with E Major on the left. On the right is the minor version: E minor.

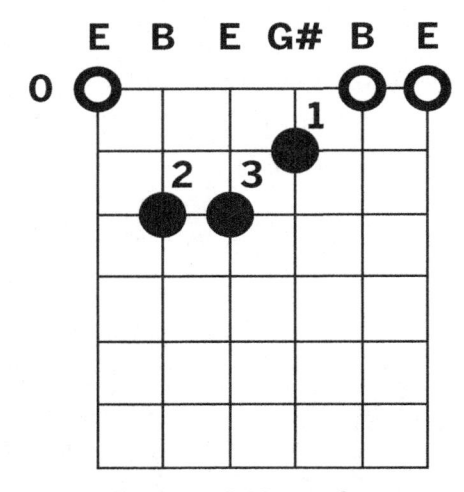

FIG.111 - E MAJOR CHORD

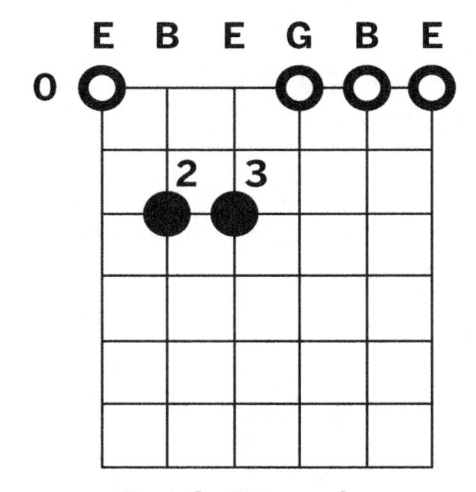

FIG.112 - E MINOR CHORD

See how there is only one note difference between these two chords? That small changes changes a major chord into a minor chord. Play the E minor version and notice the big difference in sound between it and E Major.

Generally, minor chords are used in songwriting to impart a sad feeling. Major chords, a happy feeling. Isn't it funny how changing just one note can do that?

## HOW TO PLAY A MINOR

Just as one note change converted E Major to E minor, one note changes A Major to A minor.

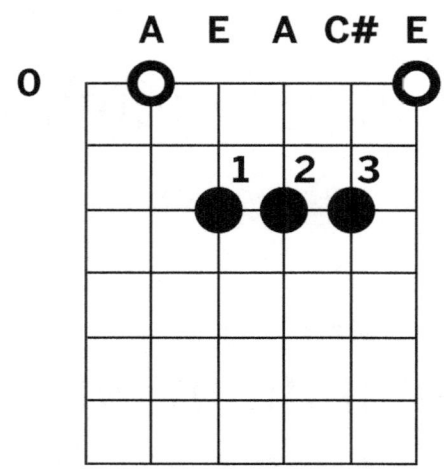

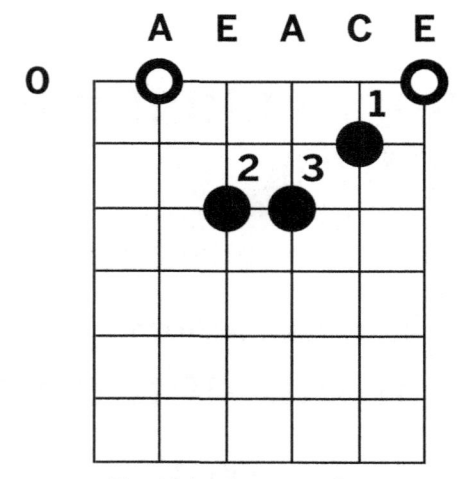

FIG.113 - A Major Chord

FIG.114 - A minor Chord

Heads up! You'll need to use a different fingering to reach A minor. Notice the fingerings in the diagram.

## PUTTING CHORD FLAVORS TOGETHER

Good music is like good cooking. It's about finding combinations of flavors that are interesting and go together well. Major and minor chords sound great together and create interesting harmonies because of their different flavors.

One chord combination that sounds terrific is C Major and A minor. Another is G Major and E minor.

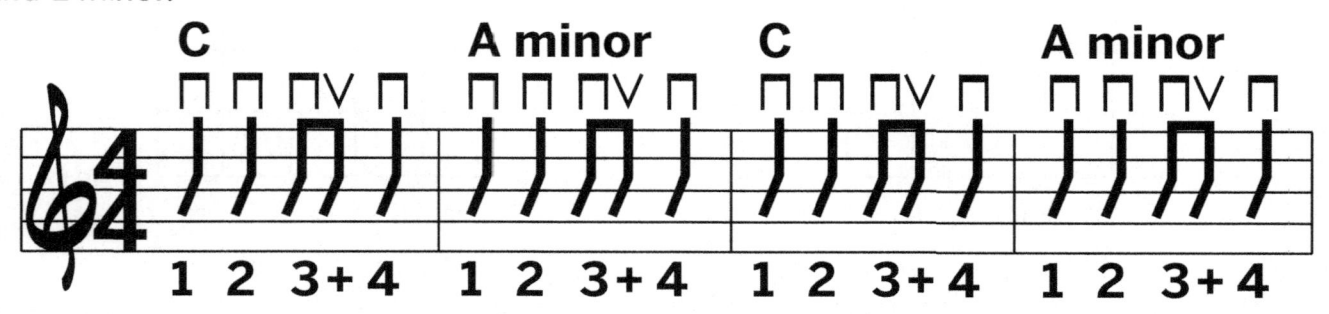

FIG.115 - C Major - A minor Progression

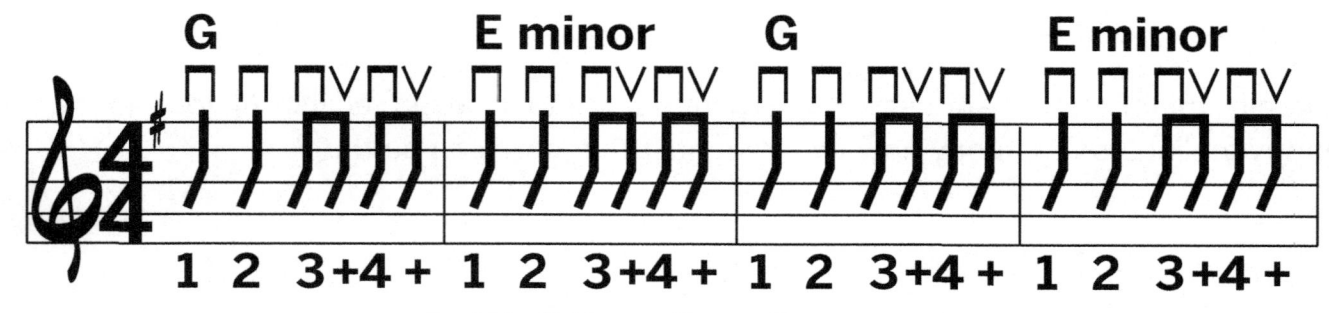

FIG.116 - G Major - E minor Progression

62 BEGINNERS GUITAR JUMPSTART: A SEEING MUSIC METHOD BOOK

Note: There are many ways to write the chord symbol for the same chord. Here are some of the ways minor chords are indicated.

$$A\ min = A^- = a$$

Fig.117 - Minor Key Naming Conventions

**Today's Assignment**

Try these progressions of chords, taking note of the different rhythms and time signatures.

Start the following chord progressions slowly at first. The goal is very steady rhythm and smooth transitions between chords, not high-speed!

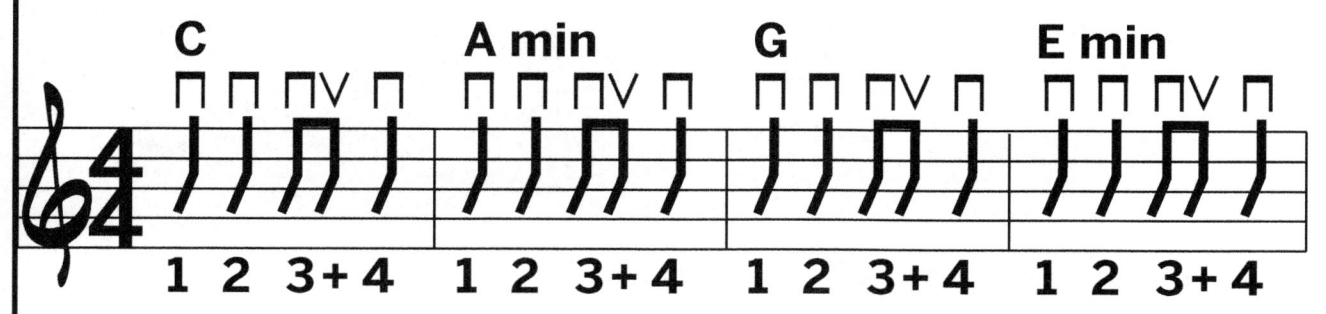

Fig.118 - CaGE Progression

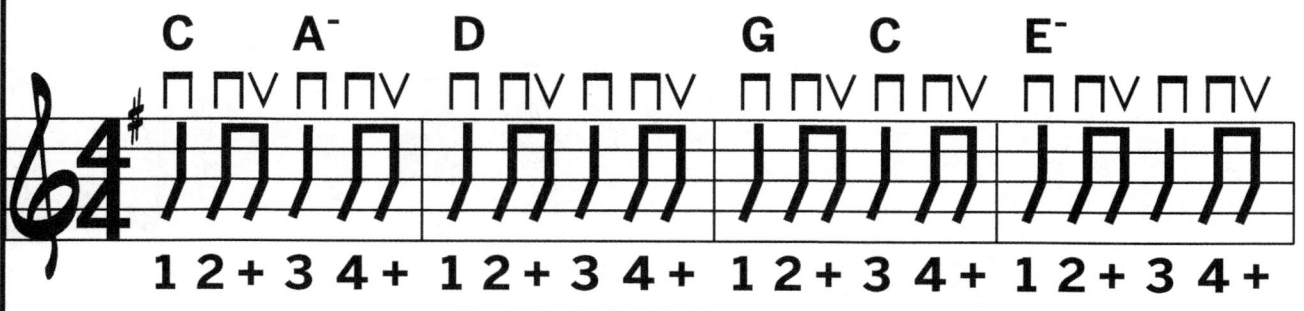

Fig.119 - CaDGCe Progression

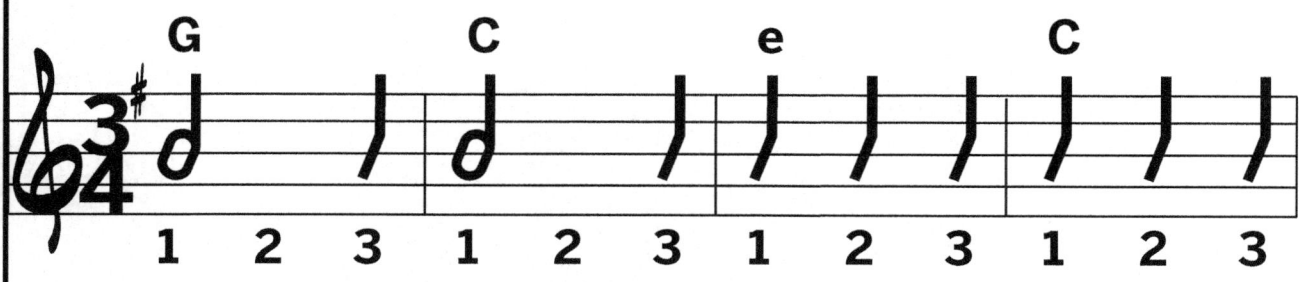

Fig.120 - GCeC Progression

**MINOR CHORDS 63**

64 BEGINNERS GUITAR JUMPSTART: A SEEING MUSIC METHOD BOOK

# DAY 10 - PLAY YOUR FIRST SONGS

## MILESTONE

**Just think of all the chords you've learned in just a few days.**

**Remember all the combinations of rhythms and time signatures you've used.**

**Time give yourself a pat on the back for assembling all this knowledge in a short amount of time!**

## HOW TO PLAY JINGLE BELLS

These are classic songs that will demonstrate the many chords and rhythms you've learned.

Play these first 4 bars of Jingle Bells with all downstrokes, 3 per measure. This is a good way to learn any song, starting with a simple rhythm. Does this section look pretty easy? Yes, it is!

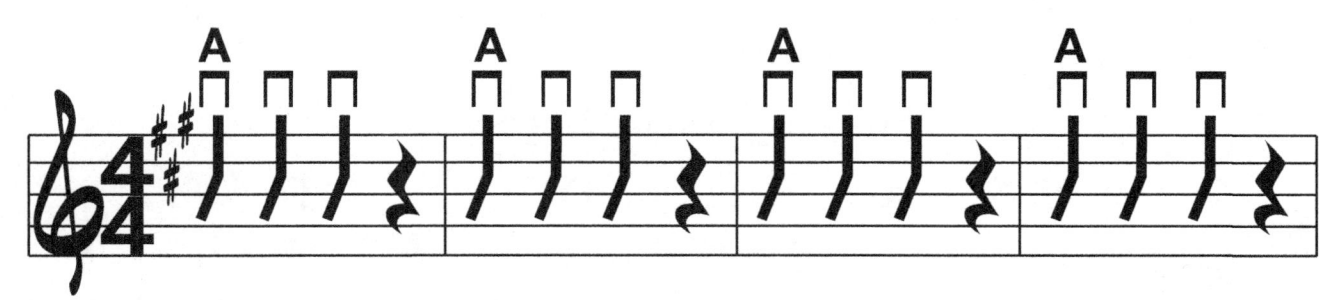

FIG.121 - "JINGLE BELLS" OPENING MEASURES

Now, here's the full song with a much more interesting rhythm. As you're getting familiar with the chord changes, feel free to substitute the more simple, all downstroke rhythm until you get comfortable.

# Jingle Bells

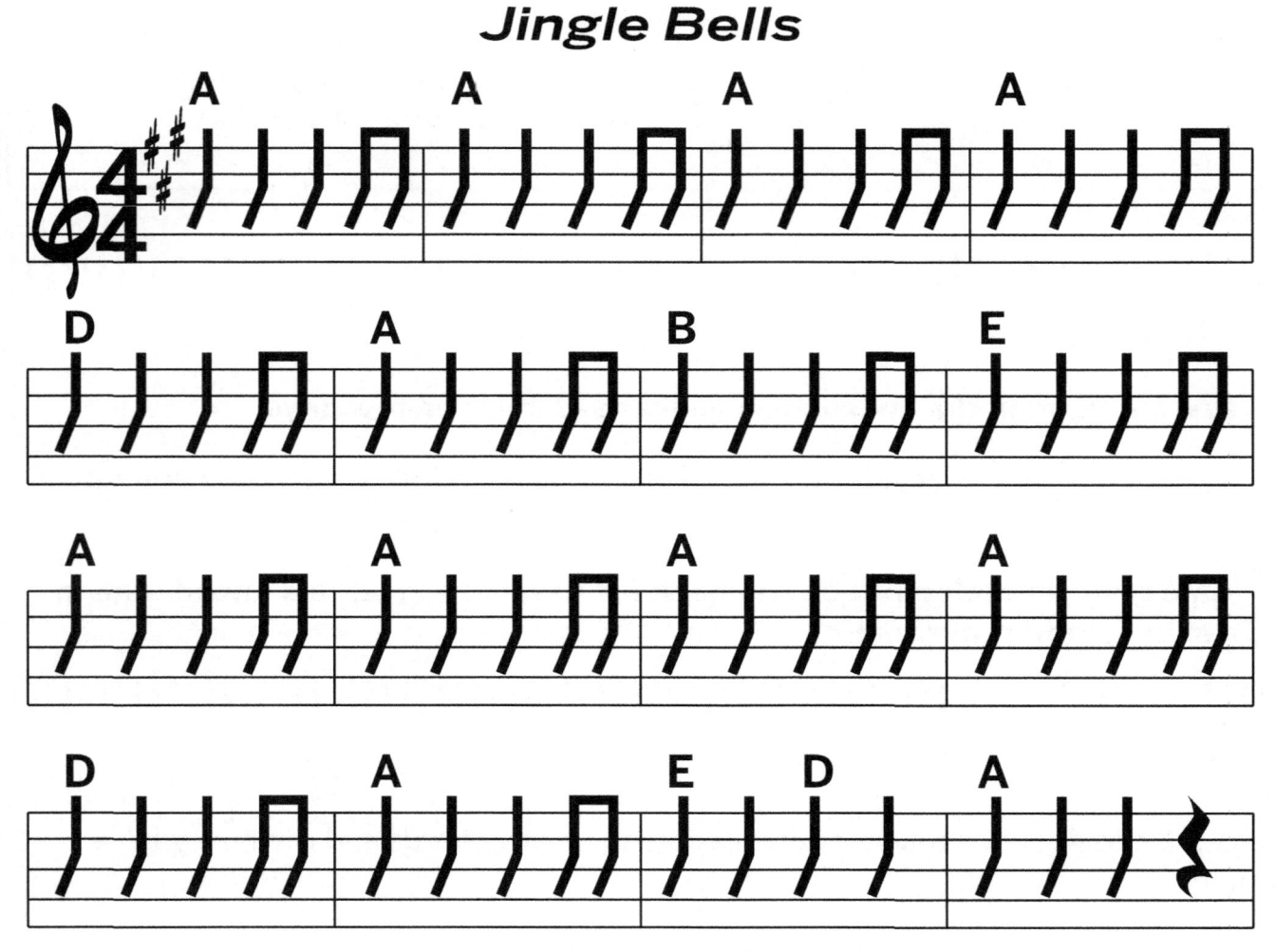

FIG. 122 - "JINGLE BELLS"

## HOW TO PLAY HAPPY BIRTHDAY

Here's a song everyone loves to hear! Again, feel free to start with all downstrokes until the chord changes are smooth and connected.

# Happy Birthday

FIG. 123 - "HAPPY BIRTHDAY"

**66 BEGINNERS GUITAR JUMPSTART: A SEEING MUSIC METHOD BOOK**

## HOW TO PLAY A BLUES SONG

Blues music is recognized and enjoyed everywhere in the world. Perhaps one of the reasons it is so popular is because it has so many varieties.

Additionally, Blues music evolved into Rock and Roll, Country music and much of Jazz. It's certainly a form worth studying!

**E Major Blues**

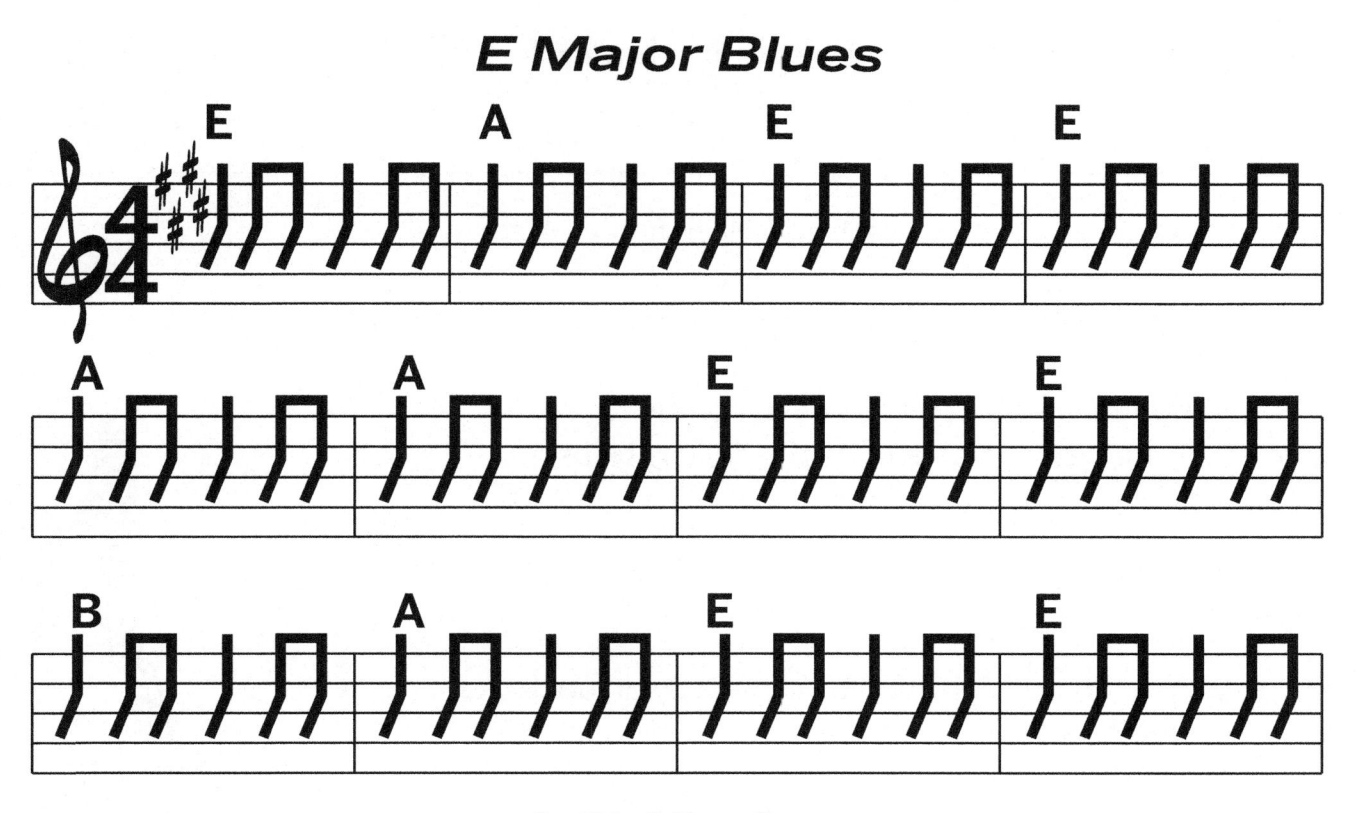

FIG.124 - E MAJOR BLUES

## HOW TO PLAY A ROCK AND ROLL SONG

Early Rock and Roll took the familiar chord changes of the Blues and started mixing things up. Often the two forms would use the same chords, but Rock and Roll would recombine them, putting a new twist on familiar chords. See how much this song sounds like the Blues.

PLAY YOUR FIRST SONGS 67

## A Major Rock and Roll

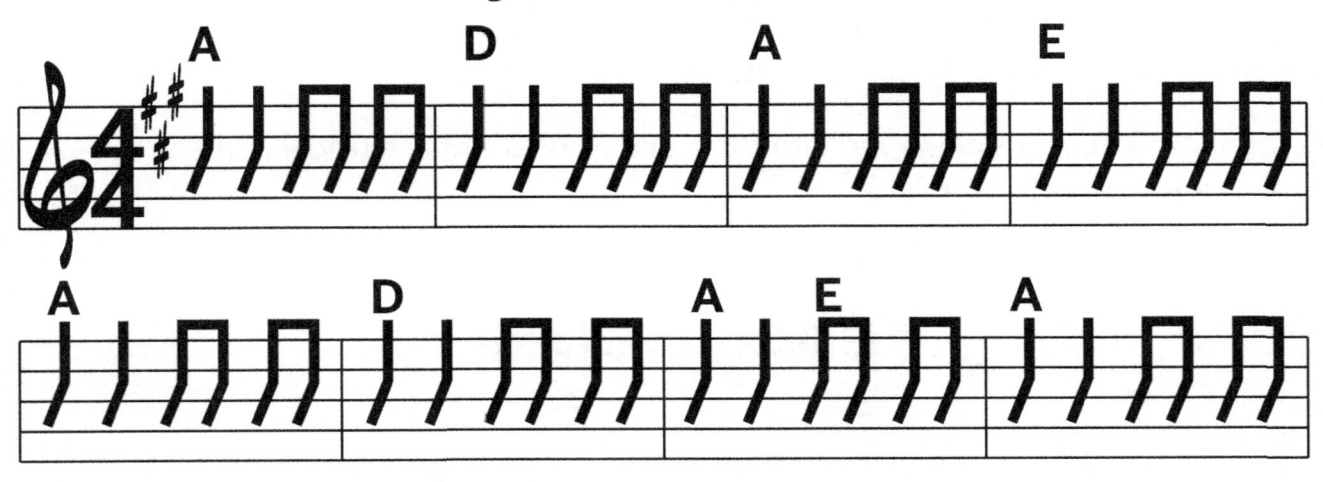

FIG.125 - A MAJOR ROCK AND ROLL

## ROCK AND ROLL WITH MINOR CHORDS

Early Rock and Roll music certainly wasn't afraid to experiment! Here's an example of 1950s-style rock using major and minor chords.

This song uses an eighth-note rest followed by an eighth-note, like this:

Play a reststroke on the eighth-rest followed by an upstroke on the next eighth-note.

## G Major Rock and Roll

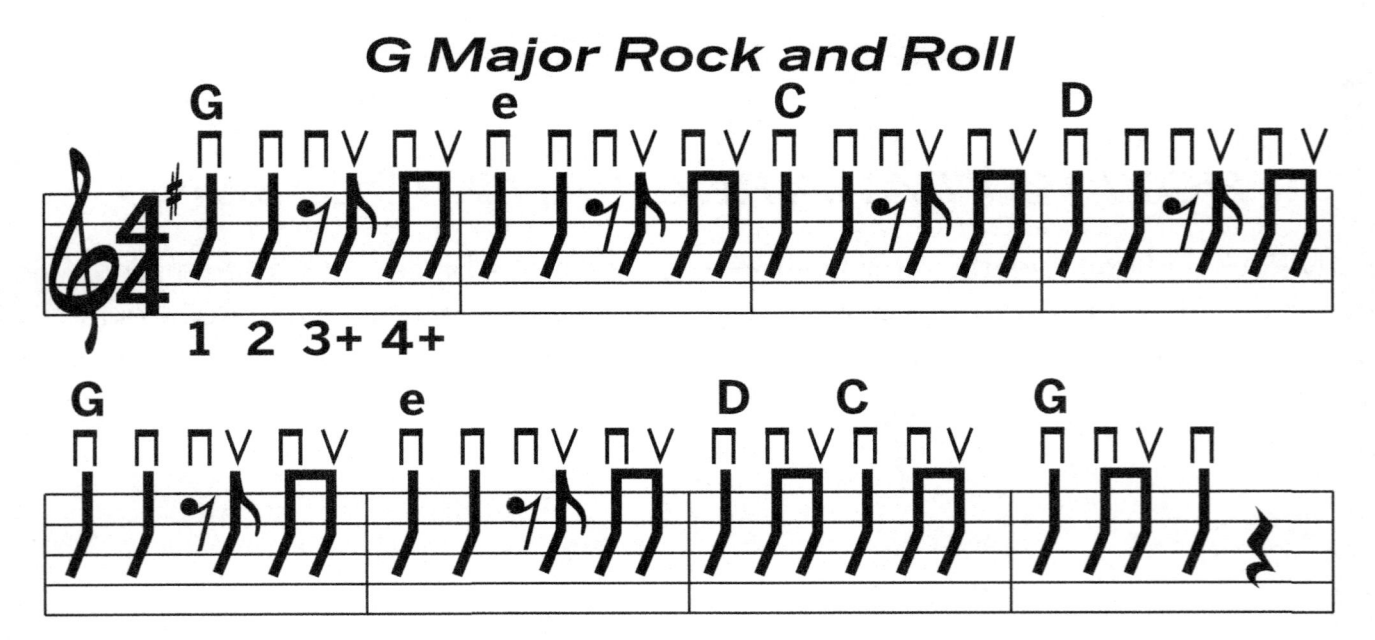

1 2 3+ 4+

FIG.126 - G MAJOR ROCK AND ROLL

**68 BEGINNERS GUITAR JUMPSTART: A SEEING MUSIC METHOD BOOK**

## Today's Assignment

Continue practicing the songs in this chapter. Then, try making up your own songs with combinations of chords and rhythms you like. Are you ready? Of course you are!

Of course, you may not like every combination of chords you try. That's normal. Write down the chord combinations and rhythms you find interesting on the sheet music below.

70 BEGINNERS GUITAR JUMPSTART: A SEEING MUSIC METHOD BOOK

# MILESTONES IN MUSIC

Time to congratulate yourself on all you've learned!

- How to read fretboard diagrams
- Note names through the first 5 frets
- Time signatures and note values (eighth, quarter, half)
- Major and minor chords
- Many commonly used strumming rhythms
- C Major and G Major scales
- Traditional, Blues and Rock and Roll Songs

## ASSIGNMENT

### *Today's Assignment*

Keep learning! You're well on your way to total guitar and musical knowledge! Explore the vast world of music and dive into everything you find interesting. You already have to tools to make music and begin answering the questions you'll discover along the way.

There are several books in the *Seeing Music* family you may find interesting to develop your knowledge and skill. *Seeing Music* books put you inside the mind of professional guitarists everywhere who organize their vast knowledge by very simple visual means. Our books give you the tools to continue teaching yourself, to be able to play anything, anytime.

Keep on makin' music, musician!

72 BEGINNERS GUITAR JUMPSTART: A SEEING MUSIC METHOD BOOK

# CHORD AND NOTE REFERENCE

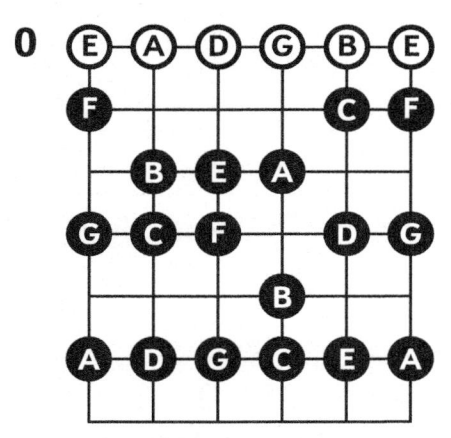

Fig. 127 - Natural Notes

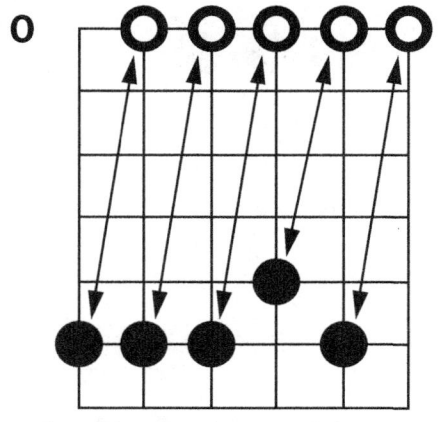

Fig. 128 - Open-string Equivalents

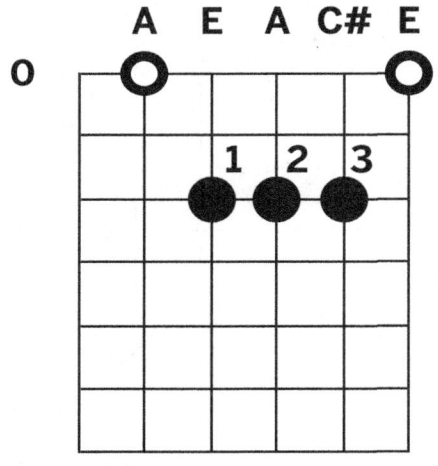

Fig. 129 - A Major

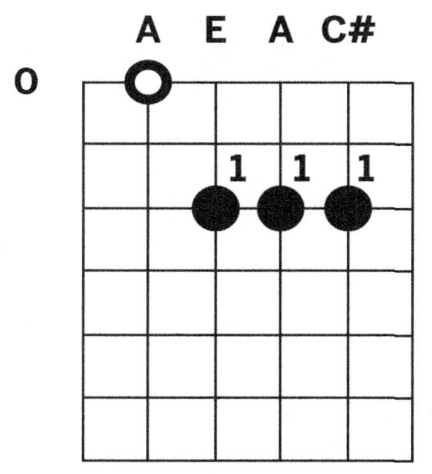

Fig. 130 - A Major Barre

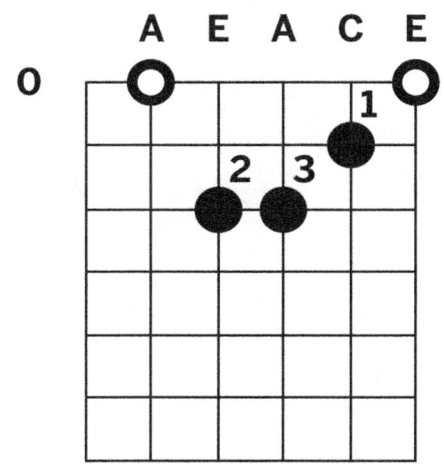

Fig. 131 - A minor

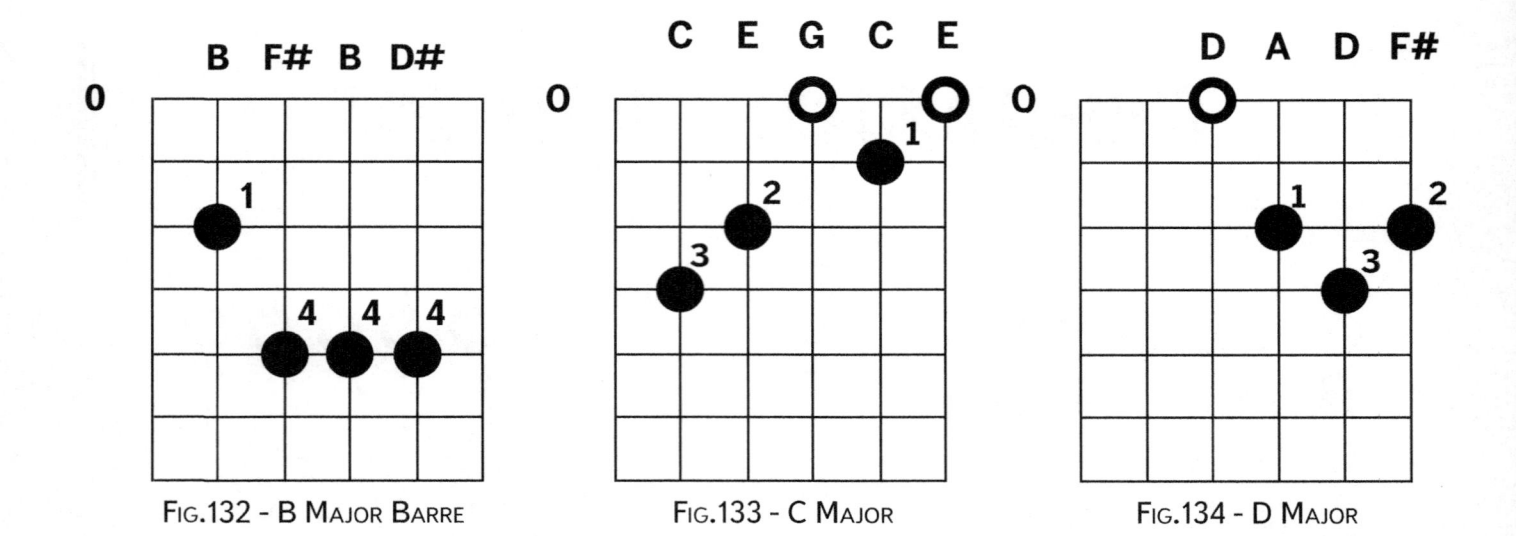

Fig.132 - B Major Barre

Fig.133 - C Major

Fig.134 - D Major

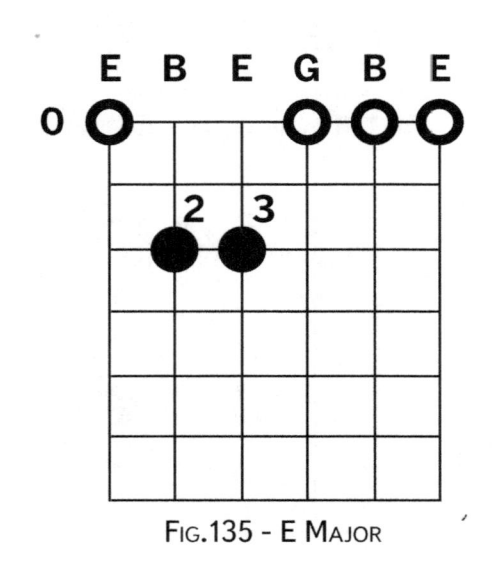

Fig.135 - E Major

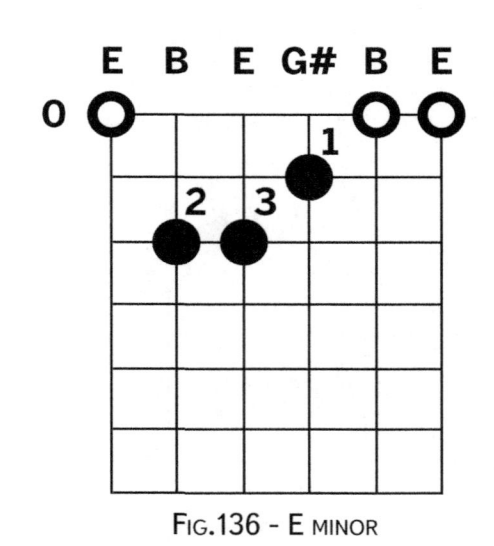

Fig.136 - E minor

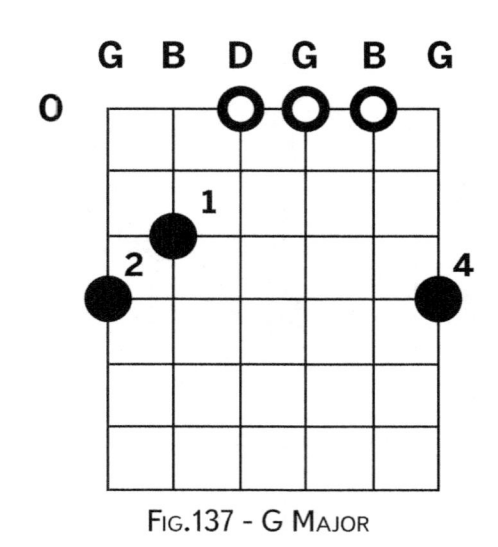

Fig.137 - G Major

**74 BEGINNERS GUITAR JUMPSTART: A SEEING MUSIC METHOD BOOK**

Printed in Great Britain
by Amazon